MW01181603

Discard

THE GREAT
HISPANIC HERITAGE

Francisco Goya

THE GREAT
HISPANIC HERITAGE

Francisco Goya

Tim McNeese

CHELSEA HOUSE
PUBLISHERS

An imprint of Infobase Publishing

Francisco Goya

Chelsea House
An imprint of Infobase Publishing
132 West 31st Street
New York NY 10001

Library of Congress Cataloging-in-Publication Data

Francisco Goya / Tim McNeese.
    p. cm. — (The great Hispanic heritage)
 Includes bibliographical references and index.
 ISBN 978-0-7910-9664-2 (hardcover)
 1. Goya, Francisco, 1746–1828. 2. Artists—Spain—Biography. I. Title. II. Series.
 N7113.G68M42 2008
 759.6—dc22
 [B]   2007032075

Text design by Takeshi Takahashi
Cover design by Keith Trego and Jooyoung An

Printed in the United States of America

Bang EJB 10 9 8 7 6 5 4 3 2 1

This book is printed on acid-free paper.

Contents

Introduction

It should have been an easy campaign of conquest for Napoleon's well-trained, well-armed troops. The self-proclaimed French emperor thought Spain might fall into his lap within one week of fighting. His forces, the Grande Armeé, easily appeared vastly superior in every way to their Spanish counterparts. To Napoleon, the Spanish were nothing, their military was "riddled with nepotism and corruption, top-heavy with incompetent officers, antiquated in organization, badly equipped, ill-trained, and small."[1] When the war between the French and the Spanish began in 1808, the entire army of Spain numbered 115,000 men, of whom 15,000 were stuck in Denmark, due to an earlier arrangement between Spain's King Carlos IV and Napoleon.

DISPARATE ARMIES

The largest problem Spain faced in its war with France was not a lack of soldiers but a shortage of money. In 1807, Spain's national income was 700 million reales. From 1807 to 1814, after seven long, bloody years of war, it had dropped to half as much. Through those years, Spain was bled dry by war.

During the early months of 1808, the call went out for all single and widowed Spanish men between the ages of 16 and 40 to take up arms on behalf of the king. Yet this only resulted in thousands of "enlistees" without the means necessary to fight. Due to a lack of funds, this ragtag army "could not be fed, shod, clothed, or even adequately armed."[2] Over the following two years, things would worsen as several Spanish colonies in the Americas revolted, depriving Spain of much-needed assets. Military conditions in Spain were terrible. For every three horses the Spanish cavalry needed, only two were available. Almost no cavalrymen had helmets. The Spanish were outnumbered by French cavalry by as many as five to one. Artillery units were forced to use cannon made out of wooden staves held together by iron hoops, which blew apart after only a shot or two. In the Battle of Leon, the Spanish actually outnumbered the French army by more than 10,000 men (23,000 to 13,000), but 9,000 Spanish soldiers had no weapons, and there was no Spanish cavalry.

Yet French dreams of conquering Spain in only one week were soon dashed. Although the French army defeated the Spanish in nearly every battle, they could not ultimately win the war they had brought to the Iberian Peninsula of Spain and Portugal, although the invaders did take control of the Spanish government for a short while.

Napoleon's military campaign against Spain could not have come at a worse time for the Spanish monarchy. Carlos IV had risen to the throne 20 years earlier and had ruled Spain poorly, allowing its army to become ineffective and disorganized.

French emperor, Napoleon I *(above)*, or Napoleon Bonaparte, had acquired control of most of continental Europe by the end of the eighteenth century. In 1808, his armies invaded Spain, and in May, citizens in Madrid, rebelling against the French occupation troops, were gunned down. Years later, the heroic uprising was captured on canvas by the great Spanish artist, Francisco Goya.

He was not very bright and was dominated by his wife, Queen Marie Luisa, to whom he often deferred to in matters of state. Carlos was physically strong, but he was not a strong leader.

ROYAL INTRIGUE

As Napoleon prepared to take control of Spain, the queen and her son, Ferdinand, quarreled over which of them should *truly* rule Spain. Ferdinand plotted against his father, but his intrigue was uncovered by perhaps the only official in the Spanish Bourbon court who had any political skills whatsoever, Manuel de Godoy. Once caught, Crown Prince Ferdinand "was obliged to grovel in apology before Carlos, who unwisely pardoned him."[3] Ferdinand repaid his father's grace by plotting against both the king *and* Godoy.

Soon, however, French armies marched across Spanish soil. To carry out his coup, Napoleon had sent his cousin, the Grand Duke Joaquim Murat, to Spain. On March 23, 1808, Murat descended on Madrid with 50,000 troops. He quickly gained control over the city and ousted the Spanish royals in the name of Napoleon Bonaparte. King Carlos abdicated his throne to Ferdinand, who entered Madrid the following day to the cheering of his new subjects. The weak Carlos and his scheming queen were generally not liked in Spain. With Ferdinand on the throne, many Spaniards believed a new day might dawn for their country. They filled the streets of Madrid, celebrating, cheering, and throwing flowers. As Ferdinand's carriage approached the Royal Palace, people laid their cloaks out on the street in honor of their new monarch.

Ferdinand was convinced Napoleon meant no harm to the Spanish royal house. He even believed Napoleon would support him as the new monarch. Ferdinand could not have been more wrong. In spring 1808, Spain was swarming with French troops. Napoleon seized the throne, giving further strength to his military posture in Madrid and throughout the Spanish countryside. He ordered the deposed Ferdinand to travel north into exile with his parents.

To make certain that Spain was ruled properly, Emperor Napoleon selected one of his own brothers, Joseph Bonaparte, to be the new king of Spain. Joseph was loyal to his conqueror-brother. He had already proven himself to be the perfect bureaucrat and national administrator by serving previously as the emperor of Naples, another region that Napoleon had conquered. Yet even before the selection of Joseph was made public in Madrid, Spanish countrymen rose up against the French.

In taking the throne from the hands of the Spanish royal family, Napoleon had intended to destroy any royal connection in Spain to the Bourbon family. The Bourbons were the royal family with long historical roots in France. The French Revolution (1789–1799) had overthrown the Bourbon king Louis XVI and beheaded him. When Napoleon came to power in 1799, he made himself ruler and emperor, establishing his own family line of royalty. He then sought to remove any Bourbon influence from his country. Carlos IV was a member of the Bourbons.

Yet Napoleon was not content to remove the king, queen, and crown prince from power. There were other Bourbons in Spain around whom the Spanish people might possibly rally. They included Carlos's 13-year-old son, Prince Francisco de Paula, and Carlos's brother, Don Antonio, and his family. Napoleon soon ordered the prince to be seized and taken across the northern Spanish border into southern France. This decision angered the people of Spain. Rumors began to spread throughout Madrid, where the people were already enraged that their monarchs had been removed not only from their thrones but from the country itself. One rumor that fanned the flames of anger and fear was that Napoleon was going to execute the royal family. Such stories spread, "multiplied by a thousand mouths,"[4] leading to a series of violent events, unfolding early in May 1808.

A STREET UPRISING

About 8 A.M. on May 2, Spanish subjects gathered at the Puerta del Sol, Madrid's main plaza, near the Royal Palace. They watched as Don Antonio and his family was led out of the palace to waiting coaches. Accompanying them was 13-year-old Prince Francisco. The sight of the French taking the last of the royal Spanish family into captivity angered the crowd. People began to shout and jostle one another. Others rushed to the plaza, and soon the scene was crowded with angry *madrileños*, citizens of Madrid. They chanted in unison, "Long live the king and our royals! Death to Napoleon! Frenchies out, out, out!"[5] Because of the early hour, the majority of those gathered in the streets were simple, working-class citizens on their way to work.

The people in the crowd soon produced weapons and anything they could get their hands on—sticks, knives, clubs, and even a handful of old guns. Fighting broke out. From the upper-story windows and balconies of Spanish houses, angry madrileños showered down everything from furniture to boiling oil on the French. A flowerpot struck the general of the Imperial Guard, killing him. The unplanned, random uprising was an eruption of frustration and fear that would shortly become an all-out riot against the French troops in Madrid. The French took swift retribution where they could, as desperate Spaniards were mowed down by French bullets on the Plaza de Oriente. Where any shots had been fired from a house, soldiers stormed in and killed all the residents. The French army rampaged through the city and the surrounding countryside. Riflemen broke down the doors of a local monastery and decapitated the monks.

Most of the action took place in the Puerta del Sol, one of the busiest places in Madrid. There, rioters fought a detachment of the Imperial Guard, including 24 Mamelukes. The Mamelukes were Egyptian mercenaries whom the people of Madrid loathed and feared for their excessive and brutal tactics. The Mamelukes were attacked by rioters. Organizing their ranks, the Egyptians charged across the square and met the frenzied attacks of madrileños, who were wielding their crude weapons. Some of the Mamelukes were dragged off their horses and killed by the Spanish. Puerta del Sol was in chaos, and casualties on both sides were extensive. Although the number is probably exaggerated, when Grand Duke Murat made out his report of the uprising to Napoleon, he claimed that "several thousand" protestors had been killed.[6]

SWIFT REVENGE

The fighting and rioting continued for two hours that morning. Perhaps as many as 200 Spaniards were killed or wounded in the rioting. The Puerta del Sol was covered with bodies. Although the rioting was not renewed the following day, the French took decisive steps in response to the spontaneous uprising. French troops began rounding up Spanish subjects whom they thought might have been involved in the riots. Hundreds were taken prisoner. On May 3, mass executions took place across the city at selected sites: the hospital courtyard next to the Church of Buen Suceso; along the Paseo del Prado, near the site where the famous Prado Museum stands today; and at the Mountain of Principe Pio, a small rise approximately 200 yards (183 meters) from the Liria Palace. The accused received no trials, and the killings were brutal. Firing squads of French soldiers cold-bloodedly gunned down the Spanish.

Not far from the Mountain of Principe Pio lived the most famous Spanish artist of the early nineteenth century, Francisco Goya. How much he saw of the rioting on May 2 is unknown. Did he witness these bloody events? Did he participate? Where was he when his fellow Spaniards were rounded up and shot down the street from his home? What did he see? What did he hear? What did he feel?

The answers to these questions remain uncertain. Yet these two days, May 2 and 3, 1808, would change not only Spain's future, but they would forever alter the career of

Francisco José de Goya y Lucientes (1746–1828) was already an esteemed court painter to the Spanish royalty and chronicler of Spanish life when the events of May 2 and 3, 1808, occurred near his home in Madrid. This self-portrait shows the artist at about 70 years of age.

Francisco Goya. Six years later, Napoleon would finally be defeated. Armies from Great Britain, Prussia, and Russia gathered against the French emperor and, after years of conflict, brought about his defeat on the battlefield and his abdication from his own throne. That year, 1814, Goya would paint two great works, *The Second of May 1808* and *The Third of May 1808*. The works portrayed the rioting, the bloodshed, and the anguished faces of those about to be executed. The canvases presented two scenes from Spanish history, two days easily overlooked by many. By creating these two monumental works, Goya would not only remind his fellow Spaniards of their valiant struggle against French oppression, but he would also lay the groundwork for modern art.

1

Vague Beginnings

Only the barest of facts are known about Goya's first 25 years of life. These early years remain little more than a vague shadow. He was born on March 30, 1746, in the small village of Fuendetodos, located near the capital of the former kingdom of Aragon, Saragossa, in northeast Spain. Saragossa was so close, in fact, that "at times a breeze would bring the sound of [its] church bells."[7] The small, simple house in which he was born, No. 18 Calle de Alfondiga, still stands today. The house was a plain cottage hut with dark, heavy stone walls punctuated by small windows.

HUMBLE ORIGINS

The town of Fuendetodos was an unimportant settlement described by an English visitor several decades after Goya's death "as a straggling hamlet with a few hundred people at the edge of a sluggish stream."[8] At his birth, Goya's hometown was "as dry as the inner lives of its inhabitants."[9] Nestled on Spain's arid central plateau in old Aragon, the town was home to just over 100 residents. Fuendetodos lacked a local river, and the annual rainfall was limited. Many in the community were poor farmers who worked the surrounding wheat fields for almost no pay. Many of these fields had formerly served as cattle pastures, but had now been overgrazed and nearly stripped bare. Life in Fuendetodos was bleak and uninspiring, a sun-burnt landscape "with only a gnarled tree or a jagged outcropping of rock breaking the low line of a featureless horizon."[10] It was hardly an environment to inspire a young artist. Yet this humble, lonely place may well have helped to form young Goya into the man he would one day become. He grew up in a gray world of poverty and rural remoteness. In turn, this may have worked to create "the darker side of his nature—his selfishness and his essential loneliness."[11]

His mother was Gracia Lucientes, whose family had a claim of undetermined Aragonese nobility. This entitled them to a coat-of-arms, although the aristocratic connection meant little. In fact, during Goya's lifetime, Spain was home to a large population of lesser nobility. Approximately 5 percent of the kingdom's people, at least 500,000 in number, could claim aristocratic roots. His father, José Goya, who also claimed aristocratic ancestors, was from a Basque family. At the time of young Goya's birth, José was working as a gilder, a low-level artist of sorts, who decorated furnishings, decorative items, and picture frames with gilt, or gold. It was a profession left over from medieval times, when craftsmen would often perform the work of artists. Times were hard for the Goya family, and José supplemented the family income by working a small plot of land that had been part of Gracia's dowry.

Although few legal or family documents exist to give much background about Goya's youth, there is a church record with his name on it. The day after his birth, his parents took him to the local parish church where the priest baptized the infant. The record, signed by Joseph Ximeno, Vicar, provides all the pertinent facts:

The small town of Fuendetodos is located in northeast Spain, not far from Goya's second home, Saragossa. This small street, with the Fuendetodos church in the background, is reportedly the one where Goya grew up.

On the 31st day of March, 1746, I, the subscribing vicar, baptized a child born on the day immediately preceding, the legitimate son of Joseph Goya and Gracia Lucientes, legally married, inhabitants of this parish, in the district of Zaragoza [Saragossa]. He was named Francisco Joseph Goya, his god-mother being Francisca de Grasa, of this parish, single, daughter of Miguel Lucientes and of Gracia Maria Salvador to whom I made known the spiritual kinship which she had contracted toward the baptized and the obligation to teach him the Christian doctrine should his parents fail to do so.[12]

A LESSER KINGDOM

Spain was an awkward nation in the eighteenth century, as it had been since it was created when two ancient Iberian kingdoms, Aragon and Castile, were joined into one. In 1479, King Ferdinand of Aragon and Queen Isabella of Castile had brought their two noble houses together and formed the state of Spain. The royal pair is best remembered for giving Christopher Columbus three ships with which he reached the Americas. Yet, while Spain was officially a single, united kingdom, for many of its people this meant nothing.

The people who lived in eighteenth-century Spain still thought of themselves in medieval terms. They lived locally, provincially, and understood little about other parts of the country that were remote to them. Historically and geographically, Spain had been divided into numerous regions by a series of mountain chains. In each of these regions—Aragon, Old Castile, New Castile, Catalonia, Leon, and Valencia—there were differences in climate, landforms, and the crops or animals on which each local economy was based. Each region had its own local color and its own local loyalties. In Spain, one was a Castilian, a Catalonian, or an Aragonese before considering himself a Spaniard. As one eighteenth-century writer noted, Spain was "a body composed of other and smaller bodies, separated and in opposition to one another, which oppress and despise each other and are in a continuous state of war."[13]

Young Goya fit into this pattern of cultural and regional allegiance. As a young man, he would have no true loyalty beyond that of his family, his village, and the Catholic Church that he was baptized into.

The Spanish kingdom, however, did exist. With the advance of Spanish colonialism into the Americas during the 1500s and even into the 1600s, Spain had become a dominating empire of great wealth and power, fueled by massive amounts of gold and silver taken from Mexican mines. In later years, however, the kingdom fell on hard times, being ruled by a string of weak and indifferent monarchs. Eighteenth-century Spain began with the death of Charles II, known by his subjects as Charles the Bewitched, the last of the Spanish Habsburgs, in 1700. Charles was prone to fits brought on by epilepsy. He was small in height and puny, disfigured from a bone disease, and mentally retarded. His tongue was so large he could barely be understood, and he drooled constantly. Unable to produce an heir, at his death the throne passed out of the Habsburgs into the hands of the Bourbon family to Philip of Anjou, also know as Philp V, the grandson of the French King Louis XIV. (Philip's grandmother was a Spanish Habsburg.)

Since he was not from Spain nor a true Habsburg, the new king was forced to engage in a war with the Austrians, another branch of the Habsburg lineage, to defend his accession to the Spanish throne. For more than 10 years, the War of the Spanish Succession (1701–1714) dragged on, with Spain becoming a bloody fighting ground. Although Philip V kept his throne, he lost lands. Gibraltar and the island of Minorca went to England, and the Catholic Netherlands (present-day Flanders), Belgium, and Luxembourg went to Austria. Philip then devoted much of the remainder of his reign fighting needless and expensive wars to control parts of Italy and to regain the Catholic Netherlands. He spent huge sums of money on his armies, while ignoring the Spanish countryside and his subjects.

A NEGLECTED NATION

Spain was a neglected sovereignty during Philip's 46-year reign. Metal from Spain's colonies in the New World was used to purchase many of the industrialized goods the kingdom needed, but they were not bought from Spanish artisans or craftsmen. Instead, these goods were purchased from English and Dutch merchants and traders. In the meantime, domestic industry in Spain floundered, with the country racked by high inflation brought on by the easy availability of gold and silver. This abundance of precious metals kept Philip from working hard to advance the level of domestic industry, allowing whole parts of his economy to languish. Entire regions of his kingdom remained unproductive. There were 17 universities in Spain, but perhaps as many as 90 percent of the students "registered as a mask for idleness."[14] Many students either lived off the food they picked up at local monasteries or begged on street corners. Even at a glance, examples of the king's neglect of Spain could be seen:

> The capital city of Madrid had no centrally organized refuse collection and no coherent street lighting or cleaning service. The police force was lackadaisical in the cities and virtually unknown in the countryside, where banditry was a well-recognized danger. This was made even easier by the fact that the Spanish road system was almost totally undeveloped. Rutted and bumpy roads not only slowed travelers, who became the bandits' prey, but also made pursuit of the thieves difficult. This lack of the most elementary services and protections was only the beginning of the national government's deficiencies. There was no systematic attempt at education by the government, little encouragement of agricultural reforms and few innovations in industrial or mercantile methods. . . . Few farmers took any interest in the intelligent management of agriculture—crop rotation and irrigation, for example—and the quality of a land none too bountiful to begin with grew worse with each passing year.[15]

King Philip V, the first ruler of the Bourbon dynasty in Spain, held the crown from 1700 to 1746. For nearly half a century under his leadership, Spain floundered industrially, socially, and militarily. The losses of land following the War of Spanish Succession that he fought greatly reduced the Spanish Empire in Europe.

By the last year of Philip V's reign, the year of Goya's birth, "Spain . . . was a stagnant, if not decadent, social organism."[16] It is not surprising that many eighteenth-century Spaniards, including Goya, considered the kingship of Spain as a crown of questionable relevance to their lives.

STORIES OF HIS YOUTH

There are many stories about Goya that have come down through the years, but whether they describe events that actually took place or not is unclear. Some stories tell of a young Goya drawing pictures on the walls of his humble home, perhaps the first sign he would one day be a true artist. While the pictures he drew as an adult often feature landscapes and backgrounds that mirror his sad village and the surrounding Aragonese countryside, there is no actual proof to back up such romantic claims.

Another story tells of a priest carrying a bag of wheat to the local mill one day and passing by the young Goya who was drawing a picture of a pig on a village wall with the blackened end of a charred stick. Impressed by what he saw, the priest asked the youth who had taught him to draw. Goya told the priest that no one had. Realizing the youth to be a talent with no teacher, the priest made arrangements for Goya to be sent to drawing school in Saragossa. Yet such a story is not unique to Goya. A similar tale is told of the thirteenth-century Italian painter, Cimabue, who spotted a young shepherd drawing a picture of a sheep on a rock. Impressed, Cimabue asked the boy if he would like to become an artist. The youth and his father excitedly agreed. In time, the young man became one of the greatest painters of the early Renaissance, Giotto. Such stories, when repeated, become more questionable with each new telling.

A MOVE TO SARAGOSSA

Fuendetodos was the family home from young Goya's infancy through his early adolescence. José and Gracia had only moved to the small, rural community after Gracia inherited her small dowry. There they tried to live out the fantasy of their nobility off the income from the estate. Things had not worked out, however. José had acted the part of the nobleman, but he and his family still lived in a ramshackle house, and José worked the fields as any other peasant might. The family moved to Saragossa between 1758 and 1760 just as young Goya was growing into his early teen years. There, José could take up his craft as a gilder. (While living at Fuendetodos, he was not allowed to practice his trade, since "noblemen" were kept from performing any "useful" work.) His fortunes did not change markedly. Throughout the remainder of his life, José struggled to make ends meet. When he died years later, his official death registry stated sadly that "he died without leaving a will, because he had nothing whatever."[17]

While life might not have improved for José and Gracia in social status and wealth, it proved an important change for young Francisco. José enrolled his three sons in the Escuela Pia, a local school under the direction of Father Joaquin of the teaching order of Escolopes. (Goya had two older brothers: Camillo, who would become a priest, and Tomas, who would be a gilder like his father.) The school was similar to many across Spain, where monks and priests served as teachers and religious guides. The Escuela Pia was little more than an adequate institution where young Goya learned the essentials of reading and writing, picked up some Latin through Roman literature, and learned simple rhetoric. José wanted his boys to have something of an education, even if the Escuela Pia was the only school he could afford.

Perhaps the most important result of young Francisco's days at the Escuela Pia was that he met a young man who would change his life forever. Fellow student Martin Zapater, "a stable, sensible fellow,"[18] would remain Goya's friend for many decades. The adult Goya would refer to Zapater in his letters as "The Good Martin."[19] In their adult years, Zapater would prove to be Goya's opposite in nature. When Goya was reckless, Zapater was controlled. When Goya was depressed, his friend Martin would help him recover. Although his friend never achieved greatness, Goya often used him as a sounding board for new ideas and inspirations. Their longtime friendship, however, would have a dark side as well. As Goya became more famous, he seemed to take delight in measuring the distance he had moved ahead in life even as Martin Zapater remained a man of little consequence. Until his death, however, Zapater remained a true friend and confidant to Goya.

SARAGOSSA: YOUNG GOYA'S CITY OF OPPORTUNITY

Saragossa was an ancient city, dating back to the first-century A.D. reign of Roman emperor August Caesar. The city had witnessed international struggle numerous times throughout its history. The Germanic Goths captured the town during the fifth century. The Moslems took it during the eight century. A century later, the Frankish king, Charlemagne, tried to extend his empire to include the city, but Moslem forces kept him out. It would be an Aragonese king, Alfonso I, who finally wrested it from the Moors three centuries later, making it his capital. The result of this international tug-of-war was that Saragossa was a city of many roots, one in which its residents could "boast that in their veins flows the blood of ancient Iberians, Berbers [North Africans], and Goths."[20]

When the Goyas arrived in the old capital, Saragossa was a prosperous community, where local trade and the arts were flourishing. Despite its relative small size, the town was known for its culture and schooling opportunities. It was also the site of religious pilgrimages. The city was filled with religious relics, including the bones of numerous Christian martyrs, most of them buried in the local crypt of Santa Engrácia. It was there, according to local legend, that "silver lamps burning all night and day strangely failed to blacken the low ceiling, nor would the smoke blacken a sheet of white paper."[21] Two of the city's great churches, La Virgen del Pilar and La Seo, were built on an ancient basilica and featured religious artwork by such second-tier Renaissance artists as Ribera and Andrea del Sarto.

2

Schooling for Life

Once Goya finished his rudimentary studies with Father Joaquin, he progressed on to another religious school, a Jesuit-run "college" in Saragossa. Goya drew the attention of his tutor, Father Pignatelli, a priest who was descended from Italian nobility. Pignatelli noted the young Francisco's drawings and believed his student to be blessed with a special gift. He proposed that Goya study art under one of the city's most important painters, José Luzán y Martinez.

A NEW TEACHER

Events moved quickly for the adolescent Goya. José Goya had connections among artists in Saragossa, and he arranged to have his son apprenticed to Martinez at age 14. Martinez was not a great talent himself, but he was the best that Saragossa had to offer. He was good enough at age 30 to become a court painter after which he opened his school. He was a popular teacher, despite his practice of teaching students by having them copy from the engravings of more talented European artists. Although he never became a first-rate artist, he was given the task of serving as an art censor for the Inquisition in Saragossa. This dreaded arm of the Catholic Church, in its constant battle against sin, blasphemy, and heresy, used Luzán as Reviewer of Unchaste Paintings, having him touch up works that left too much flesh exposed, adding "here and there a leaf, a garment, a shadow."[22]

Hour after hour, young Goya sat and copied from Italian, Flemish, and French engravings. He learned very little. Eventually, he was allowed to draw by looking at three-dimensional plaster casts of Greek and Roman busts. Only after this was young Goya allowed to draw from life and nature itself. Years later, Goya would comment on the value of such teaching, which was still practiced by painters of his day: "They confuse their young pupils by making them trace for years, with sharply pointed pencils, almond-shaped eyes, mouths like arches or hearts, noses resembling the figure seven upside down, oval heads. Ah, if they were but allowed to study nature. Nature is the only master of drawing."[23] Copying the statues of Greek and Roman sculptors provided Goya his only means of learning to re-create the human body in Catholic Spain. The conservative religious leaders of the time forbade artists from painting or sculpting using female nudes. To do so was considered a crime.

As an art student, Goya did not reveal himself as having the makings of a great artist. He did not create any important works during these years of training, and only one work existed into the twentieth century. He received a commission from the Fuendetodos church in which he was baptized to decorate a reliquary, a cabinet in which religious relics are stored. The cabinet had two doors, each covering its front half. Goya painted a set of fake curtains above the doors with cherubs holding the curtains open, along with a picture he titled *The Appearance of the Virgin of the Pillar*. Then, on the inside of the cabinet panels, he painted two pictures; one on each door, titling them *San Francisco de Paula* and *The Virgin of the Carmen*. It is not certain when the reliquary paintings were done. Some art historians have dated Goya's decorations as early as 1758 to 1760, when he was between 12 and 14 years old. Given some of the technical aspects of the work, however, especially the artist's use of light and shading, the work was probably made later, perhaps in 1763. Goya took no pride in these paintings, and there is a story that tells of him returning to his old hometown of Fuendetodos in 1808, following the Napoleonic War in Spain, nearly 50 years later. When he viewed his handiwork of the reliquary, he nearly denied he had even painted the scenes, stating vehemently: "Don't say I painted those."[24]

Even if the reliquary paintings were little more than an early effort, Goya was already taking seriously the idea of becoming a professional artist. He appears to have enjoyed painting. Becoming a Spanish artist, he knew, would give him great latitude in his life. He could work his way further up the social ladder through his art than by nearly any other means, except, perhaps, a fortunate marriage to the daughter of a wealthy landowner or state official. Yet he also knew that Saragossa was not the place where he would become an artist of note in late eighteenth-century Spain. He would have to move to the center of the Spanish art world, Madrid.

A NEW HOME IN MADRID

At age 17, young Francisco Goya set out for Madrid. As with so many other events in Goya's tumultuous life, there are dramatic stories attached to his move from Saragossa to Spain's cultural center. One tells of the 17-year-old art student having to flee quietly in disguise from Saragossa because he was in trouble with church officials for having a love affair with a local girl. Another tale puts Goya in the middle of rivalries between the parishioners of different local churches who would sometimes clash with one another during religious holy days while marching through the city streets. Ironically, those religious rivalries sometimes led to violence. One such clash led to the stabbing deaths of three young men. When the killings were investigated by the Catholic Church's Grand Inquisitor, he received a list of other young men who had led the attack. Topping that list was Goya. Before he could be brought before the Inquisition, "the turbulent youth resolved on flight."[25] While the story is colorful, there is no proof that such an event took place or that Goya was ever a wanted man

ARTISTIC RIVALS: MENGS AND TIEPOLO

Among the artists invited to create works for the new Royal Palace in Madrid were two men, each representing the two significant art styles of the day, neoclassicism and rococo. The artists were Anton Raphael Mengs and the Venetian painter Giovanni Battista Tiepolo. Mengs was the neoclassicist, a 33-year-old artist "certain that he had discovered in the classical style the one true path to beauty."* He arrived in Madrid in 1761.

Tiepolo arrived the following year, and, in his seventies, had accomplished a great artistic career with influences that spread from Italy to Germany. He was the last of the original great masters of rococo. Tiepolo used warm colors and covered large canvases with lively compositions that were free from restraints and rules. He painted religious subjects, but he also created pic-tures of pagan myths, filled with frolicking gods and goddesses. He was commissioned by Carlos III to decorate a huge portion of the ceiling of the Royal Palace. He and his two sons produced a 140-square-yard fresco called the *Apotheosis of the Spanish Monarchy*, a sprawling, cloud-filled pantheon of cherubs, mytho-logical gods, craggy cliffs, and stumpy columns.

Yet, the day of rococo had seemingly past, and the younger Mengs had his own supporters in Carlos's court. He also had a giant ego. Mengs was "overwhelmingly ambitious, jealous, hated concerning the Inquisition. It may be more accurate to say that Goya went to Madrid because it was the next natural step in his process of becoming the artist he wanted to become.

When he reached the capital, Goya found himself in a city split by two art worlds, both old and new: the neoclassical and the rococo. The neoclassical was led by a young German painter, Anton Raphael Mengs. Rococo found its chief supporter in Giovanni Battista Tiepolo, an old Venetian painter. The older of the two styles was rococo, an approach to art

---

other painters."[**] While many art historians today think that Mengs had no imagination as an artist, "an ignoramus pretending to be a scholar,"[***] Carlos wanted the young neoclassicist to paint for him so much that he gave into Mengs's vain and various demands. The king even paid Mengs's passage to Spain by providing him with a large Spanish naval vessel. Once Mengs began producing works of art for the king, he was soon elevated above Tiepolo. Carlos III appointed Mengs as the director of the Royal Academy of San Fernando.

Mengs was destined to become an important artist in his own time. His father had been so determined that his son become a painter that he took him to Rome when the boy was 12 years old and "parked him in the Vatican galleries with a hunk of bread and a bottle of water and told him to start copying."[†] Mengs copied the works before him, producing works of the Belvedere collection of antique statuary, the ceiling of the Sistine Chapel, and the paintings of his godfather, Raphael.

[*] Quoted in Richard Schickel, *The World of Goya, 1746–1828* (New York: Time-Life Books, 1968), 35.

[**] Quoted in Evan S. Connell, *Francisco Goya: Life and Times* (New York: Counterpoint Publishers, 2004), 17.

[***] Ibid.

[†] Ibid., 16.

established in France during the early eighteenth century. It was a lighter, more graceful, and entirely more playful style than its predecessor, the baroque style. As rococo was a break-away style from baroque, so neoclassicism represented an attempt to turn away from rococo. Born about the same time as Goya himself, neoclassicism recalled the pure architectural and artistic lines of ancient Rome and Greece. It stripped away the excessive ornamentation of both the heavier baroque and the whimsy of the rococo. Goya would have to choose between the two styles.

Yet, artistic opportunities did not automatically open up to Goya. He was sufficiently confident of himself to enter a competition for a scholarship to study art. The contest, held every three years, was sponsored by the Royal Academy of San Fernando, the most prestigious art school in Spain. When the prize was announced in January 1764, an anxious Goya found he had not only failed to win the grant but he had not received a single vote. More disappointing, the aspiring young artist would have to wait another three years before the next com-petition. This fact leaves a gap in Goya's biography. Almost nothing is known about his activities from 1764 to 1766. It is believed he remained in Madrid where he continued to prac-tice his art. Certainly, he had plenty of artworks to study in the city's churches where religious paintings were in abundance. He probably struggled financially, living in the poorer parts of the city. Living on little and making almost nothing as an artist may well have given Goya experiences that would later affect his art. Since many of his adult works were of economically lower-class subjects, including not just the poor, but outcasts, lunatics, and the crippled and the malformed, Goya may have had many opportunities to associate with such subjects in Madrid's taverns, flophouses, and other dens of low morality.

UNINSPIRED LEADERSHIP

Even if Goya made no progress during his first years in Madrid, the city was experiencing extraordinary change itself. By 1764,

Spain had gone without a general war for most of a generation, first under King Ferdinand VI, then under his half-brother, Carlos III, "who was perhaps the only genuinely enlightened monarch Spain has ever experienced."[26] Short in height, his skin as dark as mahogany, Carlos was a talented, gentle man, even as he was prone to depression. Despite his solid qualities, he was boring. He lived and expected his royal court to live without excess. He was not prone to drink, he hated music and going to the theater, and absolutely despised watching bullfights, one of the most common and popular activities in all of eighteenth-century Spain. Carlos, after all, had left Spain at the age of 16 and lived in Italy for the next 27 years.

Ferdinand had managed to institute several important reforms in his country. He restructured the navy, abolished the state sales tax, and provided government subsidies for such industries as mining. He ordered the construction of a modern road system as well as a canal system to encourage commerce. He encouraged the spread of the Enlightenment in Spain and sought to support the arts and literature. It was during his reign that the Spanish Royal Academy, which Goya dreamed of attending, was established. The Academy became known for producing a state dictionary to establish a standard for the national language. Some of Ferdinand's reforms and intellectual causes continued to advance and even thrive under his half-brother, Carlos III.

For Goya, who may or may not have been aware of all the king was doing to develop intellectual thought and artistic talent in Spain, the heart of his new world was Madrid itself. The new Royal Palace, a neoclassical architectural wonder with 1,200 rooms, was nearly completed after 30 years of construction. To match the splendor of the new palace, citywide renovations were undertaken. Streets were widened into boulevards, and new government buildings were constructed. The new city was even larger than the old, its limits spilling out into the former countryside. Modern street lamps were erected, a new sewage system was installed, and improved water-delivery systems were developed. An expanded and more professional police force was established as well. With the advance of Spanish colonialism into the Americas, life was full and rich in Madrid, and everywhere one could find excitement:

> Spaniards had always had an affection for the communal enjoyment of streets and squares, perhaps because of the bustling contrast of the austerity of their homes. Street fairs, religious processions, performances by strolling jugglers, even the bullfights, which often took place in open plazas in those days, formed one of the distinguishing characteristics of Spanish life. Now, with the city's streets cleaner and safer, this life became more vital than ever in Madrid. The twilight stroll along one of the great avenues—a time for flirtation, argument … relaxation and refreshment—became a custom that persists today. There is no question that Goya himself took a particular delight in the pastime.[27]

A NEW OPPORTUNITY

By 1766, Goya had his second opportunity to compete for a scholarship for the Royal Academy of San Fernando. That year's competition was to paint a scene from Spanish history depicting an earlier king of Spain, Alfonso the Wise. The rules were specific: the canvas had to measure six feet (1.8m) wide and four-and-a-half feet (1.4m) in height. Those participating had approximately six months to complete their compositions, which were due that July. Then the participants were expected to complete a second work on July 22 at the Royal Academy within a few hours. The subject was to be kept secret until that day. Goya participated, but once again he did not receive a single vote from the Academy's nine-member panel. The winner was a young artist named Ramon Bayeu, whose brother, Francisco, was a member of the jury. Francisco had been a student of Luzán's a dozen years before Goya.

Although Goya had failed again, the experience and its results taught him a valuable lesson. Spanish art, at least in

Giovanni Battista Tiepolo (1696–1770) was among the great masters of the rococo art movement of the eighteenth century. He was in high demand throughout Europe, completing major works for both royalty and the church. This fresco, or a painting done on wet plaster, adorns a palace in Venice, Italy, Tiepolo's birthplace.

Madrid, was moving quickly into the camp of neoclassicism. Goya knew he would have to learn to paint in that style or fail as an artist. Logically, who better to learn from than the artist who had just won the 1766 Academy competition, Ramon Bayeu? Goya's old teacher, Luzán, may have made the arrangements, and soon Goya was accepted as a student of Bayeu's. For the following three years, Goya, now in his early twenties, studied at the feet of Bayeu. Art historians today consider Bayeu to be a second-rate artist, and many consider his brother, Francisco, to be the better painter. The apprenticeship, however, had secondary results for Goya as well. While studying under Bayeu, he met and fell in love with Bayeu's younger sister, Josefa. They would one day marry.

INSPIRATION IN ITALY

Despite the value of his apprenticeship, Goya emerged from the experience a restless man. He felt he had not yet found his true inspiration, and he struggled for new direction. His restlessness shows itself in, again, a long list of stories about Goya's private life. Tales relate how Goya constantly walked the streets of the capital "wrapped to the eyeballs in a black cloak, face hidden beneath a slouch hat."[28] Stories tell of him standing beneath the balconies of young women, playing the guitar, a musically inclined Romeo. He also carried a sword like a latter-day Montague. He was still prone to violence, once attacking a man for mocking a hunchback, and on occasion, pulling his sword to engage an enemy following an insult. He hung out with jugglers, street people, and gypsies. He was a man of the world, finding life in the streets of Madrid. Soon, however, he was off to Italy to find new inspiration.

Little is known about his days in the Italian city-states of the late eighteenth century. Historians are not even certain how Goya managed to pay for his trip to Italy. Legend tells of Goya working as a bullfighter. It was something he even claimed as an old man, writing in letters of his days in the bullring where "he fought bulls in his time, and that with his sword in hand he feared no one."[29] He signed such letters "Francisco de los Toros (Francisco of the Bulls)." Regardless of the truth of these reports, he reached Italy by traveling through southern France, where he took the time to copy a painting by Simon Vouet and sketch works of the Renaissance painter Nicolas Poussin.

The stories of his exploits once he arrived in Italy were bound to be told. One tells of him performing as a street acrobat to support himself. In another, he received an offer from a Russian ambassador to go to the Russian capital at St. Petersburg and become the court painter for the empress, Catherine the Great. One of the oddest legends, but one that resounded with Goyaesque excess, was about a nun with whom the young artist fell madly in love. He then raided the convent where she resided, ready to whisk her off to a lover's hideaway. The scandalous kidnap led to Goya's arrest and condemnation to hang. Only the interventions of the Spanish ambassador saved Goya's neck. Again, this story is unlikely. Did he really scramble to the top of the highest of St. Peter's domes to scrawl his initials in graffiti? Did he really meet the great French painter Jacques Louis David who would become famous as Napoleon's court painter? There was never a shortage of such stories, untrue as they all probably were.

Some stories are highly likely, however. While in Rome, Goya probably met with Mengs, who was in Italy at the time due to his bad health. Goya also spent some time with Tiepolo's son, Domenico, who probably gave Goya letters of introduction to acquaintances and friends. These people opened their piazzas to show the young Spanish artist their paintings, etchings, and busts. He may also have paid a call on diplomat Don José Nicolás de Azara, who was also from Aragon and who worked in the Vatican. Through de Azara, Goya may have been allowed to view additional private artworks.

Goya's months in Italy represented more opportunity and exposure for him than the average Spanish youth of his lower-rank background could ever have in a lifetime. The works of the masters were everywhere, and he seized the advantage to learn from them. In Rome, he could not have missed the works of the great Renaissance painters such as Michelangelo and Raphael. His specially arranged visit to the Vatican would

Anton Raphael Mengs (1728–1779) was a notable German painter who was a favorite of Spain's King Carlos III. His work helped establish the neoclassicism movement of art, a distinct departure from Tiepolo's rococo style. This painting of King Carlos III is one of Mengs's most noteworthy works.

have assured him of that. In the city of Parma, he viewed the brightly painted frescoes of sixteenth-century painting master Correggio and seems to have found significant inspiration for his own later works, which often mirror the early master's style. He saw darker works, such as the prison paintings of a contemporary artist, Piranesi, again finding a touchstone for later Goya compositions. He viewed paintings by lesser-known artists, including Alessandro Magnasco and Pietro Longhi. He also found interest in some new works by Giuseppe Maria Crespi and Giacomo Ceruti that featured subjects including "common people and their life in the streets."[30] Such less formal, commonplace subjects are among those Goya would return to repeatedly during his long artistic career.

IN SEARCH OF THE ARTIST

Perhaps more important than anything else, Goya's artistic pilgrimage through Italy convinced him of his own artistic commitments. He would never be able to whole-heartedly attach himself to neoclassicism. It was too rigid and too disciplined. Its subject matter was also too limited in scope. He did not turn instead unquestioningly to either rococo or its parent, baroque, but in these forms he found something he could not in neoclassicism. They gave him a sense of being that neoclassicism could not. Through these vibrant, organic styles, Goya responded emotionally. Through them he could *feel* something.

It was during his time in Italy that Goya heard of yet another artistic competition. It was sponsored by the Academy of Fine Arts in the northern Italian city-state of Parma. The entrants had to illustrate a scene of Hannibal sighting Italy as he crossed the Alps. The piece was to show the Carthaginian ruler's march from Spain through modern-day southern France to Italy in the third century B.C. The subject for the competition was perfect for Goya. Had he not traveled over that same region on his way to Italy? One problem facing Goya, however, was that foreign competitors had to submit their works through academy representatives in the town where they were living. Goya was uncertain his painting would be given the same consideration as an entry by a local contributor, causing him to mislead the judges. He signed his work with "Goja," the Italian version of his name, and stated he was from Rome and a pupil of Francisco Bayeu, the court painter to the Spanish monarch.

Goya was heartened when he received news that his painting received six votes by the panel of judges. The winner, however, garnered seven votes, earning the prize of a five-ounce gold medal. The disappointed Goya could comfort himself with the words of the judges, who praised his work, stating "that if he had been more truthful to nature in his coloring and less eccentric in composing the subject he would have won."[31]

Whether his failure to win the competition was the reason or not, Goya soon chose to leave Italy and return home to Spain. By now, he was 25 years old, and his artistic skills were greatly improved, although he was still not satisfied. He had rejected the confining perimeters of neoclassicism, yet he had not yet fully embraced the other two obvious stylistic choices, baroque and rococo. Nor had he yet landed on a style of his own either. He felt ready to take art to another level, but where, and how? Perhaps he lacked the confidence to strike out artistically in his own direction, with his own style. Despite the bravado found in stories about Goya as a young man, including swordplay and lovesick nun abductions, Goya may not have been as confident of himself as some art historians claim. The biographer José Gudiol claims that the artist was "a timid man, governed by emotion and somewhat lacking in self-confidence."[32] Perhaps, or perhaps not, but it is certain that when Goya made his way back to Spain, he did not return confidently to Madrid to make his artistic mark. Instead, he returned to the simpler environs of Saragossa It was to be here that Goya would set out to create his artistic legacy.

3

Marriage
and Career

In 1771, Goya took up residence on the Street of Noah's Ark in Saragossa. Italy was behind him, but the lessons he had learned were not. Goya had also left neoclassicism as an artistic style. What lay ahead? Where would his still-evolving art take him? Young Goya did have a plan of sorts. He had chosen to bypass Madrid, where the direct competition of artists would be fierce, perhaps even intimidating. He would use Saragossa to build up his reputation. If he succeeded in these familiar surroundings, Madrid would, in time, take notice of him.

A FAVORABLE COMMISSION

Within weeks of his arrival in Saragossa, Goya received a commission to paint a series of works for the Sobradiel Palace, the home of the Gabarda counts. The paintings were done for the palace's chapel and included four large paintings of biblical

(continues on page 42)

THE SOUL OF SPAIN

There have, of course, been other great artistic geniuses in the history of Spain. Some came before Goya, such as El Greco and Diego Velázquez, and others such as Salvador Dali and Pablo Picasso have followed him. Each Spanish painter has lent his talent in creating a part of the canvas that is the legacy of Spanish art. With El Greco, for whom Spain was an adopted home, his legacy was to depict the "spiritual aspiration of the Spanish soul"* on canvas. He created works that the Catholic Church in Spain could accept as visions of a painter in love with his God, his church, and of the redemptive spirit of Spanish Christianity. His paintings revel in the light of theological idealism of Spain's sixteenth century.

Following El Greco, Spain's next great master was Velázquez, the seventeenth-century painter of Spanish kings, royal families, and of the splendor of the age of Spain's powerful rise on the world stage as the sponsor of Christopher Columbus. Spain was the great European power in the New World and the controller of its great wealth, embodied in the gold and silver delivered from Central and South American mines to the Spanish treasury in Madrid. Velázquez painted "Spain's worldly pride and power."**

Today, despite the significant contributions of El Greco and Velázquez, so much of the heritage of Spanish art rests on the shoulders of Francisco Goya. Perhaps most essential to this heritage is the fact that Goya always considered Spain and his Hispanic heritage as highly significant and crucial to his personal identity.

Spain was a constant inspiration to Goya. He is seen as the painter of the *true* Spain, of the worlds that Spain was beyond royal portraits and those of aristocracy. Goya presented his view of the real Spain, the common Spain. He understood it as part of the noble past and present of the land of his birth and heritage. It can be seen in the subject matter of so much of his art: This was Goya's Spain, together with blind beggars, cripples, cutthroats, lunatics, swaggering majos, flirtatious majas, dwarfs, bullfights, carnivals, massacres, picnics beside the Manzanares, Inquisitiors seeking the Devil. Much of it Goya saw through a glass darkly.***

Goya had opportunities to leave the land of his birth behind on more than one occasion. As a young man, he left Spain to study art in Italy, but once he learned those "lessons" from the great artists of the Renaissance, he did not remain on the Italian peninsula. Instead, he returned to Spain, where he would remain for nearly all of his life. There were visits to France, but Spain was essentially a part of him. It flowed through his veins and gave him his first identity. He could no more abandon the land of his birth than he could renounce his Hispanic roots.

As a result, so much of the artistic work created by Francisco Goya would manage to capture the very soul of Spain. He is there, at every twist and turn of Spanish culture during his lifetime, capturing so much of the spirit of a place and time in his art. He painted an endless number of important Spanish people: kings, queens, counts, ambassadors, royal advisors, and wealthy patrons. Goya is also there to paint great religious works that depict the essential nature and character of Spanish Catholicism. He is there, as well, painting Spanish life embodied in the common people, including everyone from a matador to a maja to a freedom fighter.

Goya is always best defined, not as a modern painter, but as a *Spanish* painter, one who takes patriotic pride in his homeland, his people, and life as it was in his own time on the Iberian Peninsula. Goya was, after all, "a [Spanish] provincial at heart."†

*   Quoted in Richard Schickel, *The World of Goya, 1746–1828* (New York: Time-Life Books, 1968), 7.

**   Ibid.

***   Quoted in Evan S. Connell, *Francisco Goya: Life and Times* (New York: Counterpoint Publishers, 2004), 102.

†   Schickel, 37.

(continued from page 39)
scenes and four smaller works, each depicting a saint. The subject matter for the larger paintings was merely taken from already existing French and Italian engravings, so Goya's originality was fairly limited. It was in his four saint pictures that the Aragonese artist revealed "a certain joyousness of spirit and technique but little else of a striking nature."[33] His works were accepted by his patrons, the commission was a success, and Goya's reputation was immediately spread further.

By October 1771, officials on the building committee for Saragossa's second cathedral, the Church of La Virgen del Pilar, the Shrine of Our Lady of the Pillar, approached Goya about a new commission. Construction on the cathedral had begun 90 years earlier. It had been built to replace a small holy shrine. Over the decades, the great cathedral had risen "majestically on the banks of the river Ebro, with its many-colored, tiled domes reflecting in the water."[34] Now, it was finally completed to the point where work on the interior art and decorations were ready to begin. Goya worked quickly, producing sketches of his planned fresco to the committee in only three weeks. Other artists competed for the fresco, but Goya won the commission. Perhaps his asking price, 10,000 reales less than his closest competitor, tipped the balance in his favor. Yet even though the committee chose Goya as the artist to paint the fresco, they wanted to submit his final sketch to the Royal Academy of San Fernando in Madrid for a professional, second opinion. When Goya delivered his second sketch, however, the building committee was so pleased that they decided not to send it on to anyone in Madrid.

Goya's fresco for the Shrine of our Lady of the Pillar would take him six months to complete. The work, *The Adoration of the Name of God*, was a baroque effort in every way, as if Tiepolo was giving him direction from the grave. There are clouds everywhere, thick and heavy, with a great angelic choir of mostly young female figures. Above them and their cloud cushions hangs a triangle, shimmering gold, and enveloped in bright light. The triangle, a symbol of the Trinity, is inscribed with Hebrew words that mean "the Name of God." The work was immediately popular with the churchgoing public, helping to solidify Goya's provincial career as the leading artist in all of Aragon.

BECOMING A SUCCESS

Not only would Goya become the most famous painter in the town of his adolescence, he would begin making money for the first time in his life. According to the city tax rolls, by 1775,

THE UNKNOWN WIFE OF FRANCISCO GOYA

Art historians and Goya biographers today know little about Josefa Bayeu Goya. Regardless of the motivations of their marriage, Goya and Josefa remained husband and wife for 39 years until she died in 1812. They would have several children through those years, although the exact number is not known. What is known is that only one survived his early years to become an adult. It appears that Josefa was not directly involved in her husband's art work or that she had any interest in that important aspect of his life at all. Her only contribution to his art was that she posed for a portrait on one occasion. In it she sits passively, her hands folded in her lap, "a slender, thin-lipped woman with large eyes, even features and reddish-blonde hair."[*] The portrait was not painted early in their marriage but several years later after "time and cares had etched her face with fine lines, and there is a distance, an emptiness, in her expression."[**] Josefa was a plain wife whose life was likely so unadorned and simple that she served to balance Goya's excesses. She ran their household, gave birth to their children, nursed and cared for them until all but one died, and was, at the end of the day, there when Goya needed her to see to things and care even for him.

[*] Quoted in Richard Schickel, *The World of Goya, 1746–1828* (New York: Time-Life Books, 1968), 39.
[**] Ibid.

Goya was Saragossa's wealthiest artist. He was still painting works for churches, but he was also painting portraits of and for some of the region's upper class, those with money and titles. As he gained in reputation, he was also creating with his style. While he did not completely abandon the baroque style, he was starting to experiment with it. This was most obvious in a series of 11 large frescoes he produced for the church of the Carthusian Monastery of Aula Dei.

Unfortunately, several of these paintings have not weathered well over the years. The monastery, located about 10 miles (16 kilometers) outside Saragossa, was being refurbished during the 1770s. By 1774, a scaffolding was erected for his work, and Goya had begun the commission. He painted these works in oils applied directly to the walls. Unfortunately, they have been damaged by humidity and by the ravages of the Napoleonic conflicts of the early nineteenth century. The church fell further into disrepair and disuse after 1836 when it was no longer used as church property. Four of the 11 paintings have been lost due to damage. Nevertheless, these works mark the end of Goya's days as an artist in Saragossa. Gone are the images of baroque artists—including an earlier Goya himself—of billowy clouds, cherubs, and heavenly choirs that he painted in *Adoration of the Name of God*.

One of the 11 paintings, *Betrothal of the Virgin*, is a good example of his new experimentation with the old baroque. To begin, those populating the large canvas have come down to Earth. They stand on various parallels of four marble steps, each having the clothing, posture, and bearing of biblical characters. Joseph and Mary are wonderfully clothed, yet not too dramatically, in the heavy drapes of robes and tunics. Everyone is wrapped in similar garments, and each is given depth through the various folds and trains. Although the billowy clouds are gone, the new billows lie in the clothes themselves. A great overhead drapery towers above the scene of holy marriage. It barely passes as a baroque work at all because it is so simple in design and composition. Simple, unadorned

Josefa Bayeu was the sister of Spanish painter Francisco Bayeu, an associate of Goya's. Goya married Josefa in 1773, and they remained together
until her death in 1812. Goya painted this portrait of his wife between
1795 and 1796.

humanity is everywhere and not a cherub in sight. Here, we see a restrained artist at work—and one who is inventing himself with each brushstroke.

BACK TO MADRID

In the spring of 1773, Goya left Saragossa and made his way to Madrid. His personal life was taking precedence over his professional life. He had decided to marry Josefa, the sister of Francisco Bayeu. He had postponed marriage for several years, but with his artistic reputation on the rise, a wife would help him even further. He had also arrived at that point in his life when he thought he could afford a wife and, perhaps, a family to follow. Whether he was passionately in love with Josefa is not certain. Cynics have implied that Goya only chose her to tie himself directly with the Bayeu legacy. In any case, the wedding took place on July 25, 1773. By becoming Goya's bride, Josefa began a life that included "the dense shadow in which she was destined to live by the side of her husband."[35]

The early days of Goya and Josefa's marriage were spent in Saragossa. Yet the couple was not to remain there for long. He took up his work on the Aula Dei paintings, but other voices were calling to him. Toward the end of 1774, Goya was summoned back to Madrid. It seems that his earlier artistic connections were beginning to pay off. Mengs had just been assigned by the Spanish crown to redirect the Royal Tapestry Factory of Santa Barbara in Madrid. He selected Francisco Bayeu as his number two man, to handle the artistic assignments for the tapestry manufactory's patrons. Bayeu selected his brother, Ramon, and Goya as two artists who would receive commissions to create the artistic sketches on which royal tapestries could be designed and woven. It would be steady work that paid well. Goya readily accepted the offer. Such an important position in Madrid could open many future doors. Of this, Goya was keenly aware.

Tapestries of Life

When Goya and Josefa left Saragossa, the Aragonese painter was 29 years old and eager to take his art to its next level. Since he was last in Madrid, he had learned much about himself and his work. Not only was Goya different, but Madrid itself was not the same as it had been in earlier years. The capital city was in the throes of modernization, trying to put some aspects of its past behind and taking a new view of the world, a view centered in the French philosophy, the Enlightenment.

AN ENLIGHTENED VIEW

The Enlightenment represented a humanist viewpoint that gave less significance to God and to the Christian religion. This view recast the Deity as the Creator and the Supreme Being, giving him credit for bringing the universe into existence, as a clockmaker builds a clock, but then placing it on the mantel and walking away from it—leaving it to run according to the laws of physics, God's laws, with no additional intervention from the One who made it. Enlightened individuals relied on scientific thought and reason for their answers, emphasizing the natural world, while playing down, or even rejecting, much that might be considered supernatural. Enlightenment advocates might read the Bible, but only for moral direction, while refusing to take seriously any emphasis given to the miraculous. Such a viewpoint and philosophy of the world would prove to be a radical departure for Catholic Spaniards who had always placed their religion and their faith at the center of their lives. Goya would come to embrace this philosophy in his life.

GOYA'S RELIGION

A significant portion of Goya's paintings were of religious subjects. Yet how religious was Goya himself? In upbringing, Goya was a Catholic. During his lifetime, being a Spaniard meant one had to have some relationship with the Roman Catholic Church. There may not have been a more important institution in Spain than the church, perhaps with the exception of the monarchy. Spaniards took their religious cues from the Spanish clergy, church doctrine, and tradition. Baptism, marriage, and even death itself were controlled by the church. The fact that the pope lived in Rome and was not a Spaniard did not matter much to Catholics in Spain. The pope did not wield the same power as in other eras, and Spanish bishops would have had more power than they do today. The church in Spain, therefore, was uniquely Spanish.

Modern writers and art historians claim that Goya was a rebellious figure, perhaps a man without religion or even an enemy of the church. These claims may not be true. Yes, Goya's paintings and sketches sometimes portray Spanish priests as greedy, immoral, or drunk; abusers of power who feed "superstitious rubbish to their flocks in order to dominate them."[*] Yet to

The new Madrid was a reformed city. Many of King Carlos III's foreign advisors were gone. The monarch had replaced them with true Spaniards, "men who could focus and direct the forces of reform that had been stirring in his country for a quarter of a century."[36] These new Spanish movers and shakers stirred up Madrid and much of the entire country. The state's currency system was reformed, and a national bank, the Banco Nacional de San Carlos, was established. There were important changes in trade policy that ended the longtime monopoly held by two Spanish cities concerning New World trade. Industry was encouraged, and those who practiced traditional craft skills were to be considered as important as any person of noble rank. A secular

recognize that priests were sometimes hypocritical or morally corrupt does not mean that Goya was antireligion.

Perhaps Goya's personal faith may be seen best through his paintings. Works that include *Christ on the Cross* were not painted by a man to whom faith could not be real or realized. Yet to Goya, a blind faith in any religion, Catholic or even the dark and unsettling black arts he became so interested in later in life, could be equally destructive if they are part of the chains that bind men and women to their lesser natures. Discerning faith definitely had its place in the life of Francisco Goya.

Goya did not rely on priests, did not attend services with regularity, and may not have even been in the custom of taking the mass. His relationship with the Catholic Church was so individualistic and unique that when he lay dying, he did not summon a priest, did not make a final confession, or did not take his last communion as was done by practicing Catholics.

* Quoted in Robert Hughes, *Goya* (New York: Alfred A. Knopf, 2003), 156.

public school system was established, ending the stranglehold the church had had over education for centuries. Related to that change, the state ordered 10,000 Catholic Jesuits, the holy order that had directed the church's education system, out of Spain and its colonies. The Spanish Inquisition, which had terrorized Spaniards for centuries, was not ended, but its powers were seriously limited.

The world of Western Europe was changing in similar ways. The Industrial Revolution, with its steam engines, textile mills, and coal-driven industries, had already begun to redefine the future, and Spain had no intention of being left behind. Carlos III was responsible for supporting, even fathering, many of these changes. He was intent on taking Spain into the nineteenth century as a modern nation. Sadly, he would not succeed ultimately. After his death in 1788, much of this reforming spirit evaporated. One Spanish writer noted the change was like "a flash of lightning illuminating us for one moment only, to leave us in greater darkness."[37]

WHIRLWIND OF CHANGE

The Madrid of 1774 to 1775 that Goya returned to, however, was in the midst of this whirlwind of modern change. Goya would find himself transported by the Enlightenment, and it would dramatically affect his approach to his art. It would provide the basic building blocks for his approach to his chosen profession:

> Until now he had been a painter developing the skills of his hand, the sight of his eye. Now he found an ideology, a faith, that gave him a new and more purposeful direction. In Madrid he learned that the basic assumption of the Enlightenment was that what was natural was right, morally and esthetically; that it was the business of intellectuals and artists to explore and define nature with a new precision; that the basic tool

they possessed for this great task was their reason. And so he became a disciple of this new, secular religion.[38]

Unfortunately, Goya's embrace of the Enlightenment would later lead him to question much of what he was ready in 1775 to take for granted. During the following generation, the Enlightenment "drove him on his expedition to the outermost limits of the human mind, whose darkest regions he mapped with his brush and pencil, and, when the Age of Reason collapsed into an Age of Revolution, he was driven to despair."[39]

Yet for the moment, little of that future mattered. Goya had an important job, and the future lay ahead of him unknown, yet inviting. He threw himself into his work almost immediately and produced the first of his full-scale paintings, which were to be translated into tapestries. Mengs and Francisco Bayeu had decided to create tapestries that deemphasized the usual biblical subjects and Greek and Roman mythologies, focusing instead on themes that promoted the simplicities of Spanish country life. It was not that Mengs was personally abandoning neoclassicism: it was that King Carlos III had developed a genuine taste for such things, and Mengs and Bayeu were working for him. The Enlightenment, too, was a motivator, since the philosophy placed much importance on nature and people living naturally, in tune with the land. Therefore, the Spanish countryside would present a broad panorama of subjects, and Goya dove into the topic fervently. By late spring 1775, he produced his first "cartoon" for a tapestry. Others soon followed. They were large works, not great works, featuring hunters and fishermen. The pay was good, even though he was not salaried but instead paid by the canvases he produced. Between the years 1778 and 1780, Goya was paid 82,000 reales for his tapestry cartoons. That compares to the salary of the Spanish court painter, a prestigious position, which only paid 15,000 reales a year.

Goya continued to paint for tapestries until 1780 when the Tapestry Factory was closed due to an economy strained by war between Spain and England.

SCENES FROM SPANISH LIFE

Despite the good pay, Goya's tapestry work proved to be a two-edged sword. On the downside, the paintings he completed were a means to an end. The end, of course, was to produce a full-size tapestry to hang in the drawing rooms of the wealthy. As for the paintings Goya produced, once they had been used to produce a tapestry, they were then rolled up and placed in storage at the Tapestry Factory. Eventually, the majority of Goya's cartoons were moved to the Royal Palace and placed in the cellar, where they remained until they were rediscovered in 1868, 40 years after Goya's death! Today, many of them are displayed in Spain's greatest museum of national masters, the Prado. The upside of Goya's tapestry work is that "it provided a significant pathway into the [royal] Court."[40]

The legacy of Goya's tapestry paintings is a mixed one. His earliest cartoons are not inspired. They were "so undistinguished that scholars long considered them works of the brothers Bayeu and other artists, until recent documentary proof established his authorship."[41] His earlier works may have suffered because Goya was not allowed to select his own subject matter, which was determined, instead, by Francisco Bayeu.

In all, Goya would paint 63 tapestry cartoons from 1775 until 1792. They fall thematically into seven series of paintings or decorative suites, each designed to fit into special rooms in the Royal Palace, or El Escorial, the Royal Monastery. The sizes of the tapestry paintings vary according to the spaces for which their tapestries were originally intended. One of the first of his tapestries created from a subject of his own was a work titled *The Picnic*, delivered to the factory on October 30, 1776. The painting is at once obviously meant to portray a simple, lighthearted scene. The setting is outdoors, but it does not

In 1776, Goya completed his cartoon of *The Picnic* for the Royal Tapestry Factory. In this piece, Goya shows his ability to capture a single moment in time, filling the scene with vitality, life, and the pleasures of eating and sharing in the outdoors.

have the studio look that some outdoor nature paintings of the period do. Across the lower half of the canvas, the viewer finds a group of five "rowdies" laying out on the ground with the scatterings of a meal just finished—dishes, platters, bottles of wine, bread, and a large cheese—laying about as well. The men are giving their attentions to a colorfully dressed woman who is selling oranges from a basket. Yet these rural picnickers are not themselves country hicks. They are well-dressed *majos*, a class of urbanites found throughout Madrid. Their class is important to Goya's expectations for the painting. A majo, as described by an English visitor to eighteenth-century Spain, was "a low fellow who dresses sprucely, affects the walk of a gentleman, looks blunt and menacing, and endeavours after dry wit upon every occasion."[42] The same English visitor wrote of the orange seller, a *maja*, the female counterpart to the majo:

> [in] language, attitudes, walk, all have in them a perfect air of effrontery and licentiousness; but if you are not overly scrupulous as to the means of exciting voluptuousness, you may find in them the most seductive priestesses that ever attended the altar of Venus; their alluring charms inflame the senses of the wisest, and promise at least pleasure if they do not inspire love.[43]

Goya's majos and majas are lower-class dandies and temptresses who make up an entire class of Spanish society. They are freewheeling, freespirited, prone to excess, dressed to party, and ready to enjoy one another's company. Both were proud people, the majas being known for their quick speech and saucy charm, who often worked as street vendors, selling everything from oranges to chestnuts. The majos were often strong men who worked as butchers, blacksmiths, tanners, innkeepers, and, occasionally, smugglers or petty thieves. Perhaps, Goya's painting is telling the viewer that, while the maja is offering an after-dinner dessert of oranges, it may be "that it is not only oranges that she is offering."[44]

Goya would return to the subject of majos and majas in his tapestry paintings more than once. As for this work, it is rich. The composition is balanced in elements and colors that include vibrant golds, browns, blues, greens, and segments of interrupting reds. The upper half of the composition is much less crowded with people, picnic remains, a dog, and the undistracted folks who dwell in the painting's background. Soft leaves of various greens and yellows fill the scant trees that occupy the empty spaces on the landscape while an azure sky shares the horizon with thick, full clouds that are not overly baroque but natural to the eye. The scene is light and airy, with a bearing of eighteenth-century Spanish sexuality. All the details of the work, especially Goya's working of the textures, drapings, and colors of the majo's and maja's clothing, show this work to be a wonderful example of Goya's tapestries at his creative best. The tapestry would hang in the dining room of the Spanish prince and princess in the Prado Palace.

Ultimately sharing the same royal dining hall was another Goya tapestry, *Fight at the New Inn.* Measuring more than 12 feet (3.6m) in length, Goya used this cartoon to depict a common rural scene, a country roadside inn where all humanity was welcome. Commanding the painting's center is a group of coach drivers and muleteers, all from their individual corners of Spain. They have converged on the inn, bringing with them their regional stereotypes of one another—stereotypes that erupt into a fight. A half dozen men, each wearing the costume of his part of the kingdom, struggle with one another. The violence does not appear threatening or criminal but comical instead. As one pulls on the back portion of another's waistcoat, a third participant, his lower legs covered in white ankle stockings held up by blue ribbons, yanks on the ear of a fourth combatant. A fifth fighter shouts skyward, as a sixth, the most menacing of the picture, approaches the fray with a scraggly root in his hand, ready to whack the first combatant, closing the circle of mayhem and frivolous jealousy. Another pair wrestle across the ground as dogs watch intently, barking their contributions to the struggle. The painting is darker than *The Picnic,* for the light is cast through a thin, orange sunset, unlike the noonday light of the first painting. It is all fun, silliness, and bourgeoisie caricatures that shows a slice of ordinary life on the back roads outside Madrid. Goya is depicting little more than a low comedy, but the composition is clear, clean, and enjoyable.

Goya's tapestries are filled with these sorts of scenes—simple, rural, natural, and pedestrian. In one, four youngsters play together; two in a cart, while the other two play a drum and a trumpet. Another depicts a "seated doctor warming himself before an open brazier with his books near him, and two students behind."[45] There are scenes of laundresses, children on seesaws, matadors, musicians, a boy riding a ram, finely-dressed men, and beautiful young peasant women. There are scenes of popular feast days, bedchambers, and revelers alongside the Manzanares River in Madrid. In one of the most famous of the tapestry cartoons, a circle of young women, perhaps majas, hold a blanket, amusing themselves with tossing a fully dressed mannequin of straw into the air. The tapestries form an array of characters, stereotypes, and denizens, depicting the joyful and the sad, the rich and the poor, the young and the old. It represents life as Goya saw it at the time.

MEETING THE KING

Even as Goya's work with tapestries continued off and on until 1792, his career took a significant turn by 1779 when he met the Spanish king, Carlos III, as well as the crown prince and his wife. Goya had the opportunity to show them four paintings, kiss their hands, and feel fortunate he was meeting the most important members of Spanish royalty. He immediately began to dream of quick advancement. He applied within months for a position as one of the Painters to the King and was disappointed when he failed to get it. The royal denial that was delivered to Goya's sponsor and petitioner, the duke of Losada, admitted Goya's obvious talent but also noted "there not being any great urgency nor any notable dearth of painters to execute the works offered for royal service,"[46] it might

Goya painted *Christ on the Cross* as part of his application to the Royal Academy of San Fernando in 1780. The artist shrewdly chose his subject carefully, knowing that it would be popular with the Academy and that it would also attract the interest of potential patrons who could further his career.

be just as well for Goya to continue to work for the tapestry manufactory.

The sting of the royal brush-off was lightened the following year when Goya was accepted as a Fellow of the Royal Academy of San Fernando. For that appointment, he had painted a work he was certain would please the Academy. Taking a Francisco Bayeu study, which Bayeu had copied from Mengs, Goya painted *Christ on the Cross.* The painting accompanied the artist's application to membership in the Academy. The timing of his appeal to the Academy was crucial for Goya. On March 15, 1780, the Royal Tapestry Factory closed its doors. Goya was suddenly an unemployed artist. He applied to the Academy, quickly, on May 5.

GOYA'S *CHRIST ON THE CROSS*

The painter, in part, chose his subject because he knew it would be a popular one with his Academy audience. It qualified as a historical painting, which was the "category most revered by the Academy."[47] In approaching his subject, Goya chose to avoid the lighter, contemporary subjects that had filled his tapestry cartoons, as well as the color palette he had relied on for depicting his children, majas, innkeepers, and street people. He uses few colors in painting a pale, thin Jesus with hands extended upward and away from his body. Jesus is not quite suspended on the cross because Goya places Christ's feet on a wooden platform that juts out horizontally from the blackness that surrounds him. Similarly, the cross itself is vague, appearing as a dim T-frame. Jesus almost appears as if he is resting against it rather than dangling from it. A thin slip of drapery covers Jesus' loins, but the focal point of the image is his face. His head is raised in muted agony, and his eyes are rolled upward as thorns prick his forehead, producing thin, yet vivid, brushstrokes of blood. Large, heavy nails pierce his hands and feet but there is no blood there. There is no bruising and no pierced torso. Goya's crucifixion is an understated execution, yet the sharp contrast of Jesus' white skin to the black background captivates the viewer. Goya's technical skills are clear to the viewer and must have also been clear to the members of the Academy committee.

Acceptance to the Academy was a triumph for Goya, making his return to Madrid a great success. Ironically, he would not remain in the Spanish capital much longer. Just four days after his election to the Royal Academy, Goya contacted his old friend Zapater in Saragossa and informed him he had received a commission to paint the domes of the new cathedral, El Pilar. Within two months, he was making plans to return to Saragossa to take up work in the church he had first worked on 10 years earlier. By early fall 1780, Goya left Madrid, returned to his childhood town yet again, and was at work. The project he began would not go well, however.

5

"The Enlightened Ones"

Between his election to the Academy in spring 1780 and his return to work in Saragossa, Goya and his wife had a child, Xavier, "a very beautiful boy."[48] The arrival of his son gave the artist great personal joy. Professionally, he was equally satisfied. Goya returned to Saragossa with a sense of status and of artistic independence. He considered himself answerable to almost no one, not even Francisco Bayeu. He was creating new styles of painting that fit him like a glove, and this new project at El Pilar would give him "an excellent opportunity to prove his new independence of spirit.[49]

BACK AT EL PILAR

A new set of frescoes needed painting at El Pilar. The new cathedral had three domes and their adjacent walls, all bare and ready for decorating. Yet Goya had not been summoned to work on the dome paintings alone. The Bayeu brothers,

Francisco and Ramon, who had been working for years on the construction project, were also there. Soon Goya's new ego caused him to clash with the two brothers. Goya was reported as "being haughty, proud and intractable in his dealings with [Francisco] Bayeu, who was, after all, the director of the project."[50] The two Franciscos quarreled. Perhaps feeling that Goya's new artistic skills were a threat to him, Bayeu delayed acceptance of Goya's sketches to the cathedral's building committee. Disgusted and angry, Goya prepared to quit the project. Then he received a letter that would change everything. It was from a friar at the monastery of Aula Dei, whom Goya had befriended when he worked on that earlier project. Brother Salcedo's note was a gentle rebuke of the volatile Goya. He admonished the temperamental artist that "there is in man no more noble, Christian and religious act than to humble oneself to another when reason and God's law ask it."[51] The friar reminded Goya that Bayeu had the building committee's ear and respect and that Goya was in a fight he could not win. To Goya's credit, the letter changed his attitude. He remained on the project, submitted new sketches as Bayeu had requested, and by May 1781, finished the work he had been prepared to abandon.

His ceiling fresco, *Virgin, Queen of Martyrs*, was clearly superior to those the Bayeu brothers had been working on. Goya's patience was at an end, however, and he demanded payment from the committee for the work he had completed. The artist was paid, but the committee stripped him of his additional projects on Aula Dei, handing them off to the Bayeu brothers. The committee then added a fresh insult by awarding the brothers and even their sister, Goya's wife, with silver medals. Goya soon left Saragossa in disgust. He would later pen his feelings, claiming, "On remembering Saragossa and painting I burn alive."[52]

Once again, Goya chose Madrid as his destination for new opportunities. Carlos III announced a contest in which seven artists would be chosen to decorate the Church of San

Francisco el Grande. Goya vowed not only to compete but to win the commission over all his competitors. If this happened, he speculated, the next natural step was to be appointed as Painter to the King. By the following September, his sketch for the competition was selected. Goya would be one of the painters for the San Francisco church.

By August 1781, Goya was at work on his first sketch for the church, the *Preaching of San Bernardino*. He shortly presented it to the state official who was supervising the project, José Moñino, count of Floridablanca, whom Carlos III had chosen as his prime minister in 1776. The king, in fact, turned increasingly "to more moderate but hardly less enlightened men for counsel,"[53] including Floridablanca, Pedro de Campomanes, and Gaspar Melchor de Jovellanos.

FRIENDS IN HIGH PLACES

Floridablanca and his friend Pedro Rodriguez de Campomanes would both come to play significant roles in Francisco Goya's life. Campomanes was an important leader of Spain's Enlightenment. He was a forward-thinking lawyer, an economist, and most importantly, an advisor to the king. He was the leader of the *ilustrados*, which means "the enlightened ones." His close associate was Jovellanos, who was one of the most liberal officials in the king's court. He was well respected as an economist, as well as a poet and reformer, earning him the title of "the most eminent Spaniard of his age."[54] These men were the new movers and shakers within the Spanish court. They promoted the expansion of domestic business and industry and helped to establish Spain's national bank, the Banco Nacional de San Carlos.

The prime minister approved the work, and Goya completed the painting the following year. It was installed in the church on January 11, 1783. Almost a year passed before the king finally made a visit to the church, but he was pleased with what he saw and congratulated Goya personally. Although the project and the royal response took years, it was a triumph

Goya's 1783 portrait of Count Floridablanca is considered his first important portrait commission. Goya was very disappointed that the count, a high-ranking royal official, was unimpressed by the finished piece. The artist has included himself in the painting, something he often did, holding up a canvas for the count's approval.

for Goya, who so wanted to receive the approval of the royal court. Goya also achieved another important coup in January of 1783. That month, Prime Minister Floridablanca commissioned him to paint the Spanish official's portrait.

Goya was ecstatic. In a letter to his old friend Zapater, he wrote, "Although Count Floridablanca has advised me to say nothing, my wife knows, and I also want you alone to know, that I am to paint his portrait, which can be of great advantage to me."[55] Goya poured himself into the commission. At first, the project went well. Floridablanca posed for the artist, and in another letter to Zapater, Goya excitedly told his friend: "On this day I have put in the head of the portrait . . . in his presence and have succeeded in getting a good likeness and he is very content."[56]

A DISAPPOINTING PORTRAIT

Goya tried to do everything he could to satisfy the prime minister. The royal official was not the most handsome of men, yet Goya did not want to smooth over the realities of the count's appearance. Instead, he emphasized the grandeur of Floridablanca's title and importance. He painted him in a brilliantly red, gold-trimmed satin suit, a gold medal prominently on display at his chest. At Floridablanca's left and in the background is an anxious royal official, pen in hand, as if waiting for official words from the prime minister that must be committed to parchment. Goya even included himself in the portrait, at Floridablanca's right, holding up a canvas for his subject's approval. Everywhere, across the portrait, Goya included books, official documents, charts, and maps, all denoting Floridablanca's interests and responsibilities. In the backdrop, the artist placed a portrait of the king. Perhaps oddly, Goya illuminates his painting so that only the prime minister is well lit, with every other element presented in muted shadows. With seemingly every fold of his clothing gilded, Floridablanca almost shimmers, his blue eyes sparkling with equal brilliance. It is a reasonably painted work, grand in intent, but "lacking in passionate objectivity."[57] It appears that Goya, who may have been nervous through the entire process of painting the portrait, is simply showing the count his technical skills, even as he is trying to flatter his subject.

In the end, the portrait of Floridablanca, which stands as one of his first official portraits, did not bring Goya the immediate recognition and praise he sought from this most important of royal officials. The count posed when needed, and Goya received much support from Floridablanca's wife during the project, but in the end, the prime minister almost seems to have chosen to overlook Goya. When Floridablanca finally viewed the finished portrait, he matter-of-factly said to the anxious artist, "Goya, we will clear this up later."[58] What exactly the prime minister meant remained a mystery, for he and Goya never discussed the portrait again. In fact, Goya was never paid for his work. A disappointed Goya wrote yet another letter to Zapater: "Everyone is astonished that nothing should have come from the Minister of State. If nothing comes from that direction, there is nothing more to hope for; and the disappointment is so much the greater when one has had such great hopes."[59]

NEW DOORS OPENING

Despite the cool response by the prime minister to his portrait, doors soon were opening for Goya. It appears that Floridablanca introduced Goya to the king's youngest brother, the Infante Don Luis de Bourbon, who would become a new client for Goya. In a way, Don Luis was a secondary figure in the Spanish court. His life story is a mixed one. He was appointed a cardinal in the Catholic Church at age 10, only to surrender those responsibilities as an adult because he could not bear remaining celibate. He finally married at age 35, in 1776, choosing the beautiful Dona Maria Teresa de Vallabriga, who hailed from a noble family from Aragon. (Don Luis had been denied a marriage with anyone of importance in the royal family line, possibly to keep his heirs out of line to inherit the monarchy.) Don Luis was also not allowed to bring his bride to live in any of the royal palaces, so he spent his married life living outside of Madrid.

Goya was invited to spend several weeks during fall 1783 at Don Luis's residence at Arenas de San Pedro, situated on the south slope of the Gredos Mountains, 50 miles (18 kilometers) outside Madrid. He and Don Luis went hunting, and the Infante shared his hobbies, which included botany, with the artist. If Floridablanca had acted cool and aloof with Goya, Don Luis was a hearty companion and supporter. Goya and his wife spent an enjoyable time in the mountains. In another

GOYA'S PRIVATE LIFE

By the 1780s, Francisco Goya was finding his place in the realm of Spanish art. He was on his way to becoming the famous artist of his destiny. Yet what of Goya's own family? How do they fit into his world at this time? Goya and his family lived "in one of the oldest and most charming parts of the city"[*] at No. 1 Calle del Desengano, in the steep quarter of northeast Madrid. It would be his home for 45 years, until 1824, when he moved to France. He moved only once during those decades, to the second floor of another house across the street at the corner of Calle del Desengano and Calle Valverde.

In 1784, Goya's son, Xavier, was born in the house at No. 1. Of all the Goya children, Xavier was the only one to survive into adulthood. Already, several children born to Goya and his wife had died at birth or while still quite young. Other than Xavier, only one other child lived long enough to be baptized. (It was a common experience in 1700s Spain for parents to face the pain of premature child death and miscarriage.) Josefa miscarried frequently. In addition, Goya's father and sister, Rita, died in 1781.

[*] Quoted in Jeannine Baticle, *Goya: Painter of Terrible Splendor* (New York: Harry N. Abrams, Inc., 1994), 44.

letter to Zapater, Goya states, "His Highness behaved very graciously, I painted his portrait, his wife's, the little boy's, and the little girl's with unexpected success, [as] four other painters did not succeed."[60] So supportive was Don Luis of Goya and his work that he gave the artist 20,000 reales. He gave Goya's wife a gown, "all in silver and gold,"[61] The house servants told Goya that the gown was worth 30,000 reales.

When Goya and his wife left the mountain estate of Don Luis that fall (after returning a second time), the Infanta, Don Luis's wife, Dona Maria Teresa, paid the artist 30,000 reales for a pair of paintings, probably the *Portrait of Maria Teresa Vallabriga on Horseback* and the wonderfully executed *Family of the Infante Don Luis*, which is considered to be one of Goya's masterpieces. Before their October farewell, Don Luis asked a favor of the Aragonese artist. He requested that Goya paint a portrait of his favorite architect, Ventura Rodriguez. Goya agreed and produced a portrait worthy of his talent as a portrait artist. While he had produced the Floridablanca portrait awkwardly, Goya appears to have surmounted his anxieties. His portraits of Don Luis's family and of the architect Rodriguez are fluid, the work of a highly skilled and confident artist.

The painting of Don Luis's family is Goya's first major group portrait. It is crowded with 14 men, women, and children, including the artist himself, who is tucked in the lower left corner, half lit and nearly unseen. Given the crowd of subjects, the work is quite complex. The composition falls back on earlier European examples, such as the English school and William Hogarth, whom Goya was familiar with through prints. The Spanish artist Diego Velázquez may also have been an inspiration for the work through his most famous of royal portraits, *Las Meninas (The Maids of Honor)*. Goya's painting features the Infanta's immediate family, several domestic servants, and Don Luis's personal secretary and other assistants. Goya places Dona Maria Teresa at the painting's center, sitting informally at a table, as a servant attends to her unadorned

In 1784, Goya painted *Family of the Infante Don Luis*, a piece that marked the beginning of his celebrated career as painter to the Spanish royal family. The family seems content and relaxed, sharing a moment presumably before bedtime, when the children are up late and enjoying the company of the adults. Once again, Goya places himself in his painting, almost as if studying the happy family before returning to his work on the canvas.

hair. She is wearing a shimmery, gilded dress, which is muted in candlelight and partially hidden under a white shawl. At the painting's far left, two female servants stand, staring straight at the viewer, while holding a tray of accessories for Dona

Teresa's hair. Don Luis sits at his wife's side, ready for a game of cards. He is dressed in a simple house coat. Directly behind him, at the painting's left, are his son and daughter. (In 1800, the daughter, Countess Chinchon, would sit for another Goya work, which would be one of the artist's best and most beautiful portrait paintings.) There is a third youth, held by a nursemaid standing to Dona Teresa's left.

The painting is at once an extremely intimate one. Goya takes his viewers into the aristocratic family's front parlor, it seems, shrouding everything in darkness after the fashion of a well-painted Rembrandt. The room is filled with family and friends, all interconnected, all dependent on one another. Yet at center is the long-married couple, Don Luis and Maria Teresa, simply depicted and unassuming; he the banished king's brother, and she, the unacceptable marriage partner, kept from court. Goya has paid them homage even as the court holds them at arm's length. It is a sympathetic portrait, rich in half-light and warm colors. Everyone appears relaxed, a scattering of contented smiles denoting comfort and acceptance. All is right, and Goya is there, capturing it all for posterity.

A YEAR OF NEW SUCCESSES

Less than a week after the birth of Xavier, Goya scored another triumph. King Carlos III finally unveiled the altar paintings for the Church of San Francisco el Grande that included Goya's contribution, a work featuring St. Bernard preaching. Goya was there that day, and the painting was well received. Again he wrote a letter to Zapater, expressing his joy: "I have had good luck with my St. Bernard, according to the judgment of the audience as well as that of the general public. Without reservation, they are all for me."[62] The year 1784 brought other successes. Goya received commissions to paint more portraits of nobility as well as four paintings for the church of Calatrava College, located in western Spain. (Those works would be destroyed during the Napoleonic Wars a generation later.) He painted *The Annunciation* for

San Antonio del Prado in Madrid at the request of the duke of Medinaceli. The duke's family was one of the most important in all of Spain.

Goya's career continued its upward advance in the following year. He was introduced to the marquis and marquise de Penafiel, the future duke and duchess of Osuna, and the meeting would have a long-range impact on Goya's future. They would become his patrons for the next 30 years. The marquise de Penafiel, who was also the countess of Benavente, was considered "the most distinguished woman in Madrid, for her talents, worth and taste."[63] Despite her marriage to a first cousin who was not too bright or energetic, she was known for her keen wit, sophistication, elegance, and constant drive. She could read Spanish and French equally well and was known for her fine singing voice. She was an expert horsewoman, loved to attend bullfights, and reveled in conversations spent with matadors, poets, writers, actors, artists, and intellectuals. The marquise was also a supporter of the Enlightenment. She even gave lectures on the new science of the day.

After meeting the marquise de Penafiel, Goya became her favorite painter. In 1785, he painted portraits of both her and her husband. It was his portrait of her that helped "establish Goya as the best portraitist of his age."[64] *The Countess-Duchess of Benavente* is a straight-forward work, with no hidden meanings, no artful symbols, and no clutter. She stands, every inch of her body covered in hat, gloves, and gown, except for her face, which is pale and sadly pretty. The painting reveals the countess's lively, intellectually driven personality. She stares ahead, with a slight smile of the long bow that is her mouth. Colors blend from face to fabric, for the painting is as much about her clothing as anything. There are ribbons and bows, silks and fine stitchery, and flowers and fans. She is drenched in pinks, creams, blues, and yards of lace. Goya has painted his patron as femininely as possible, yet she is not a coquette. She is a worldly woman, ready to hear what you have to say.

Yet she is discerning in her judgment and far above her social peers.

With patrons like the count and countess of Benavente, Goya was in a position to advance himself further. In early February 1785, he made application for the position of Deputy Director of Painting at the Academy of San Fernando, the royal school that had passed over his paintings in competition 20 years earlier. He received the post on May 4. The year 1785 was a whirlwind of advancement, new connections, and successes, marred only by the death of Don Luis. Goya's career was going places, and fast. The following year would be just as productive.

Goya had reached the point of his full talent potential. His works were fully developed technically and stylistically. He was setting a new course for Spanish art. His talent, as it remained all through his life, was fluid, adaptable, and capable of change that was brought on by new circumstances and the people who gave him support. This phase of his life was one of relative contentment, when his art conveyed the charm of years of peace and prosperity. The peace was not only his own but that of his country. Spain was not at war yet, but in the years ahead, when war did reach his country, Goya's peace and that of his countrymen would be shattered.

6

Clouds of Revolution

Everything seemed to be going Goya's way. During the mid-1780s, Goya's income reached new heights. He had made significant bank investments earlier in his career, and his income from those as well as from his position at the San Fernando Academy amounted to somewhere between 12,000 and 13,000 reales annually. By summer 1786, he was appointed as Pintor del Rey, Painter to the King, which carried an additional salary of 15,000 reales a year. (This was a prestigious position, just a step below that of the royal court painter.) With his newfound wealth, Goya purchased a small, two-wheeled English carriage, called a cabriolet, "all gilded and varnished, which people stopped to look at."[65] It was a sporty little model, one of only three in Madrid. Unfortunately, on his first ride through the countryside, the carriage overturned, and Goya emerged with an ankle injury, a small setback. (He continued to drive the carriage for another year, but then he purchased a four-wheeled carriage that was safer because it was pulled by a pair of mules.) Goya's star was on the rise.

NEWFOUND DIRECTION

Goya was soon busy with his new assignment as royal tapestry painter. (The Tapestry Factory he had painted for earlier in his career had closed in 1780, only to reopen in 1783.) He was in charge of the program and was its creative director. By summer 1786, he was commissioned to work on a series of tapestries for the El Pardo Palace dining room. Goya was about to produce a wonderful series of six works of extraordinary spirit: *Spring, Summer, Autumn,* and *Winter* as well as *The Wounded Mason* and *The Poor at the Fountain.*

These works would preoccupy Goya until the following year. Their scale provided Goya with ample space to express his extraordinary vision of subject matter. His four seasonal paintings ranged in size from six feet (1.8m) by nine feet (2.7m) to nine-feet (2.7m) high and 12-feet (3.6m) long. He divided the subject matter for these four works into two categories. *Spring* (also known as *The Flowergirls*) and *Autumn* (*The Vintage*) depict two scenes taken from the lives of the upper class. *Spring* depicts a country scene of early seasonal greenery with girls gathering flowers. A smiling man stands behind the eldest, ready to surprise her with a small bunny. *Autumn* shows a father, mother, and small child inspecting the grape harvest on their estate, with workers gathered in the vineyard that is spread across the painting's background. Both paintings revel in the leisure that makes up the lives of the wealthy. They are pleasant in color, as the azure, pink, and white skies of Spain dominate. All is contentment, even if the female worker resting a basket of grapes on her head in *Autumn* appears slightly weary.

By juxtaposition, the paintings of *Summer* (*Harvesting*) and *Winter* (*The Snowstorm*) depict the lower classes. *Summer,* a gigantic painting measuring 12 feet (3.6m) in length, presents hay harvesters taking a break from their labors. They rest on the hay, and children are playing with abandoned hay forks. It is a well-composed tableaux of working class Spanish men, painted largely in muted tones of gold and brown. Perhaps the weak aspect of the painting are the two horses. Other than bulls, Goya seems to have never been very good at portraying animals. By comparison, Goya's *Winter* is stark and bluish gray, showing five struggling travelers crossing a winterscape that is bleak and windswept. Goya may have remembered the harsh winters of his native Aragon in creating the work. Of the five travelers, only one peers out at the viewer, from beneath a dirty white shroud, yet his glance is as chilling as the wintry universe in which the five wanderers are trapped. *The Wounded Mason* and *The Poor at the Fountain* are equally bourgeoisie in subject, the first featuring two workers carrying their comrade, a mason who has been injured on the job. The other, *The Poor at the Fountain,* shows a trio of lower-class mothers and two sons taking water from a local well. The mother is melancholy, and the face of the only son turned toward the viewer is forlorn. Whether these scenes accurately portray the respective subjects is of no matter. When Goya painted these works, intended for royal consumption, the Bourbon rulers of Spain "were reformers who believed that by presenting an optimistic view of ordinary people's lives, picturing their happiest moments, one could encourage a rise in living standards."[66]

During the winter of 1786 to 1787, Goya also painted several portraits, including the count of Altamira and King Carlos III. His portrait of the king, an ugly man, appears stiff. This is probably because, even at this point in his career, Goya was still nervous among such royalty.

By spring 1787, Goya was on the move again, heading to Alameda, the rural villa of the duke and duchess of Osuna, where he was to deliver seven paintings he had done for their drawing room. The works included popular rural subjects, such as a village procession, with its aqua overtones and

In 1788, Goya painted *St. Francis of Borgia and the Impenitent Dying Man* to decorate a chapel in Valencia Cathedral. The appearance of the demonic forms hovering near the pain-wracked sufferer hints at many of the "darker" elements that were to appear in Goya's later work.

quick brushstrokes signaling the impressionism of the next century, and a coach under attack, featuring guns, swords, knives, and a bleeding victim. Goya also rendered favorite scenes found in bedrooms across eighteenth-century Europe, such as *The Swing* and *The Fall from a Donkey*. One of the lightest of these works was *The Greased Pole*, which according to Goya's own notes, depicted "a maypole on the village green with boys climbing up it to win the prize, consisting of chickens and cakes in the form of crowns hung on the top of the pole."[67]

AN ARTIST IN DEMAND

The work was piling up for the Aragonese artist, and Goya was receiving further commissions from King Carlos III. There were life-size renderings of three saints for the Convent of Santa Ana in Valladolid, north of Madrid. The following year, 1788, brought even greater commissions, including two works ordered by the duke and duchess of Osuna (the former marquis and marquise de Penafiel). The two paintings were to depict an ancestor of the duke and duchess, St. Francis of Borgia, and the works were intended to decorate a chapel in Valencia Cathedral. The couple paid Goya handsomely, 30,000 reales for each painting. Of the two paintings, *St. Francis of Borgia and his Family* and *St. Francis of Borgia and the Impenitent Dying Man*, the latter is the most important. In the work, the saintly Francis awaits at the deathbed of a dying man. It was not an uncommon scene in the European art world of the eighteenth century, but Goya's work is different. A trio of macabre demons attend the dying man, shrouded in a reddish glow that mocks the aura of a halo around the saint's head. They are more than menacing, with their demon wings, barred fangs, and eerie, glowing eyes. According to the story on which the painting was based, the demons win the conflict between the man of God and the Prince of Darkness. What is telling about the picture is that it represents the first time Goya includes in his work such demonic figures. It would be an image he would return to repeatedly in later years in his "black" paintings.

By this time, Goya had already passed into his early forties and he once wrote how he "had grown old with lots of wrinkles."[68] Yet he was soon at work on a painting that would become one of his standard masterpieces. In a letter to Zapater in spring 1788, he writes of a commission for the prince and princess of Asturias, who resided in the El Pardo Palace. The painting was for their bedroom, and Goya was nervous about it, since he knew "the king is to see it."[69] The artist considered the subject he had been assigned to be a difficult one. He was to paint "the meadow of St Isidore on that Saint's day, with all the activity that generally accompanies it in this court."[70]

A VIEW OF MADRID

Until about a generation ago, *The Meadow of St. Isidore* (also known as the *Festival of San Isidro*) was considered a later work of Goya's, thought to have been done at the end of the 1790s. Yet that dating was based on the style Goya used in creating his work. Unfortunately, Goya moved back and forth in styles at times, making some dating estimates difficult. The cartoon Goya produced for the planned painting was immense, the largest cartoon he ever produced, measuring nearly 25 feet (7.6m) in length.

Had it ever been painted at its full size, the viewer would have been bowled over by its scope. The scene was panoramic, with the meadow on the opposite bank of the Manzanares River from Madrid, where hundreds of celebrants are gathered, spread out across the giant canvas, alongside their various carriages and picnic canopies. In the painting's foreground, up on the gently sloping ridge above the meadow, are dozens of well-dressed aristocrats. The men wear knee pants and tricorner hats, while the young ladies are in their spring dresses, holding dainty parasols that shield them from the muted spring light. In the background, across the river, is the capital itself, a shimmering city of white, dominated by palaces and churches.

Goya poured himself into the project, admitting in a letter to Zapater that "I neither sleep, nor am calm, until finishing it."[71] Although the large canvas was never painted, Goya did complete a smaller version of his composition, measuring 18 inches (45.7 centimeters) in height and approximately 3 feet (.91m) in length. This smaller work is a stunning piece, painted with a limited and muted palate, everything done with obvious and impressionistic brushstrokes. It is a wonderfully balanced and enticing painting. Art historians can only wonder if the simplicity of the elements would have been translated into something quite different had the larger painting been produced. Yet it was not painted for one reason: on December 14, 1788, King Carlos III died, and the Pardo Palace would cease to be the home of the new monarch.

A NEW MONARCH

As the future of the *Meadow of St. Isidore* was changed by the death of Carlos III, Goya's future also changed. The prince and princess of Asturias, now King Carlos IV and Queen Maria Luisa, would subsequently rise to the Spanish throne. Within five months, in April 1789, Carlos IV appointed Goya to the rank of Pintor de Camara, Court Painter, a position

THE LITTLE BOY IN RED

Goya is often remembered for his portraits of royal officials and important aristocrats and their families. In fact, Goya was among the best of the Spanish painters when it came to creating likenesses of the young, and he seems to have enjoyed painting children.

There were times when painting the famous and powerful made Goya uncomfortable, perhaps caused by feelings of inadequacy due to his humble beginnings, or simply because of his perceived need to please these clients. With children, however, Goya was relaxed and at ease. In them, "he saw not the heir to a royal throne or ducal residence, but a real child, with natural petulance, or a delight in toys."* Perhaps Goya took emotional comfort in their presence, since all but one of his own children died in infancy or while still quite young.

Children may be found in many of Goya's paintings of whole families, where those young subjects were typically secondary figures, posing in the shadows of their important fathers and mothers. Yet some portraits are of children alone. One of the most famous of Goya's portraits of a single child is his painting sometimes referred to as the "little boy in red." Don Manuel Osorio de Zuniga was the son of the duke and the Aragonese artist had first applied for 13 years earlier. Goya was soon swamped with so much work on behalf of the monarchy that he would complain in a letter to Zapater of having no time for himself and his other interests. Yet he was making more money than ever, and he was soon looking to purchase a house in Madrid, ready to plunk down 100,000 reales to pay for it.

The importance of changing monarchs in Spain nearly shrinks by comparison to the significance of other events that would soon engulf much of Europe. In 1789, political change was beginning to sweep across France. That spring, the first

duchess of Altamira. When the boy was approximately three or four, Goya was commissioned to paint the boy's portrait.

Goya's canvas featured the small, black-haired child, dressed in a brilliantly red, one-piece outfit, known as a skeleton suit, along with golden slippers, lace collar, and a broad sash with an oversized gold bow. The child seems uncomfortable posing, as most three- or four-year-olds would while being sketched for a painting. Yet Goya has included some comforts for the boy. At the boy's gilded feet is a birdcage filled with his feathered friends. Manuel holds a golden string tied to a magpie that seems unrealistically unaware of three lurking cats to the boy's right. The cats wait, the eyes of one wide open, for their opportunity to pounce on the pet they view as prey. If symbolic, the animals represent "the terrors of the world which will all too soon spring from the shadows and introduce the child to the anxieties and dreads of adulthood."[**]

[*]   Quoted in Jeannine Baticle, *Goya: Painter of Terrible Splendor*
      (New York: Harry N. Abrams, Inc., 1994), 61.
[**] Quoted in Richard Schickel, *The World of Goya, 1746–1828*
      (New York: Time-Life Books, 1968), 85.

efforts that would extend into the French Revolution were underway. Soon, the king of France, Louis XVI, became concerned about the direction and scope of the ever-expanding challenge to his power and even to the future of the French monarchy itself. Although word of the revolution was officially kept from the Spanish people themselves, the royal court in Madrid watched these events with keen interest. After all, Louis XVI and Carlos IV were blood relatives, first cousins. Quietly, Louis sent a request to Carlos: should the revolution threaten to overtake him, he would like to seek refuge in Spain. Unfortunately for the French king, he was never given the opportunity. He would be taken prisoner by revolutionaries, held in prison, tried for treason, convicted, and then sentenced to die by the guillotine in 1793.

Carlos IV hoped such revolutionary elements would not find their way into his conservative kingdom. While immediate revolution did not spread to Spain, the events in France would one day threaten Spain in other ways. The revolution continued from 1789 until 1799, during which time the French monarchy was destroyed (Queen Marie Antoinette, Louis's Austrian wife, was beheaded in 1795), even as political extremists threatened to destroy even the very fabric of traditional French life. By 1799, the revolution petered-out as a pathetic failure for the moment, only to bring the military dictator Napoleon Bonaparte to power. He reestablished a monarchy of sorts by declaring himself emperor, even as he pursued his imperial dreams of European domination. As his armies marched, they found their way to Spain, where the king was forced off his throne. All would not return to normal until 1815, with the end of the Napoleonic Wars and the exile of Napoleon to the remote island of St. Helena in the South Atlantic. Through that entire quarter century, from 1789 until 1815, Goya remained at work in Madrid, a witness to the changes brought to Spain, yet always managing to serve whomever might be in power.

Goya created this cartoon, *The Straw Mannequin*, as part of a series of tapestries that were to decorate Carlos IV's royal palace, El Escorial. The game of tossing a puppet in a blanket originates in carnival festivities and has a long history in Spanish art. Many observers believe the painting can be seen as an allegory of women's domination over men, a theme that repeats throughout this series of Goya cartoons.

REVOLUTIONARY EVENTS

Yet even as revolution was unfolding to the north of Spain, changes were soon rocking the Spanish monarchy and government, some of which would directly affect Goya. For one, uncertain of the events in France, the Spanish court seems to have been so distracted that it lost interest in continuing the decorating of the royal palace. Production of tapestries ground to a halt. Goya began receiving fewer commissions, as Spanish nobles "carefully [guarded] their incomes."[72] Goya managed to squeeze out a commission to paint a work for the altarpiece of a church in Valdemoro. During this temporary dry spell, some of Goya's friends received important titles. Zapater was made a nobleman in Aragon in fall 1789, and Cabarrus was made a count in December. Despite this advancement for Cabarrus, Queen Maria Luisa began making trouble for some of Goya's most important and long-standing benefactors and supporters, including Floridablanca, Cabarrus, and Jovellanos.

According to historians, Queen Maria Luisa would hold much of the real power over Spain although her husband held the throne. King Carlos IV was uninspired and uninspiring, "a dull and loutish fellow who delighted in bellowing his courtiers into submission."[73] One of the king's favorite pastimes was wrestling with stable servants. Carlos and his new queen had never been favorites of Carlos III, having "ceaselessly plotted against the old monarch, who had kept them on a tight financial rein."[74] This new queen dominated her husband. Maria Luisa is portrayed as a scheming woman with strong sexual appetites. She had a lover, probably several, her favorite being one of her bodyguards, Manuel Godoy. She would appoint him and others to important positions in the Spanish court as favors.

Things began to unravel for Goya's friends in less than a year following the ascension of Carlos and Maria Luisa to the throne. Cabarrus was arrested on no obvious charge on June 25, 1790, and locked away in solitary confinement. Jovellanos had already been sent away from the royal court, banished for all practical purposes. When he returned to Madrid to speak on behalf of Cabarrus, Jovellanos could not even gain a royal audience. For seven years, he was a nonperson to the king and queen. Goya himself was not safe, and on July 17, was ordered to "go and breathe the sea air" in Valencia, a veiled way of letting the artist know that he was no longer needed in the court.[75] The trip may have been fortuitous because at that time, doctors were advising Goya's wife, Josefa, to get out of Madrid and enjoy the rural air.

By December, however, Goya was asked back to Madrid. (During the months he was away from the court, he had painted a portrait of his friend Zapater.) Yet the court he returned to had a different climate. The king was uncertain of how to act with him, having been told that Goya was not particularly interested in serving the court of Carlos IV. That claim had been asserted in Goya's absence by another artist, jealous of Goya's success.

Soon Goya was busy with work, painting royal portraits, including those of the archbishop of Valencia, the countess del Carpio, and Maria del Rosario Fernandez, an actress. Goya was the darling of the royal court, busy as a painter could be. This caused Goya to neglect his work for the Tapestry Factory. When the director of the factory complained to King Carlos, however, Goya was soon back at work supplying cartoons for new wall hangings.

NEW TAPESTRIES

By May 1791, Goya completed his cartoon for *The Wedding*, intended as a huge tapestry that was to adorn the king's study in El Escorial, the palace he much preferred over El Pardo. The work featured an unfortunate marriage of convenience. The bride is a young beauty, while the groom is wealthy, but old and ugly, even grotesque. Goya placed the groom at the painting's center, juxtaposing his rather dark skin against the puffy white clouds that are set against a Spanish azure sky. The entire scene is framed by a stone bridge, which is painted to appear as if it leads to nowhere.

Perhaps the groom is a mixed blood, maybe someone from Spain's New World colonies. Yet he is out of place; dressed in fine clothes, but in a costume that is woefully out-of-date. The crowd by which the couple passes is not well-wishers but mockers who smile knowingly and even jeer at the buffoon whose only fortune is that he is taking a bride of great beauty. The painting was meant to amuse Carlos IV, who enjoyed those types of works, even if the more rigid Carlos III had not. Yet Goya may also have had a more serious intent with the painting. There are three dominant figures occupying the painting's foreground: a boy at left, standing atop a cartwheel; the youthful bride at center; and an older man on the right. The three are representative of the three ages of man—childhood, vibrant youth, and old age. The work is wonderfully curious, with its mismatched bride and groom, jeering audience, and dirt-brown stonework that heavily frames the marriage event.

Another cartoon done for this new series of tapestries was titled *The Straw Mannequin.* Goya did the work in 1791, and it would be one of the last of Goya's works intended for the Royal Tapestry Factory. It was reminiscent of a tradition carried on in Spain at that time on Ash Wednesday. The practice was to take a life-sized dummy made of straw, dress it in street clothes, hang it along the main street of a community, and then take it down just before sunset and toss it in the air. In Goya's large, vertically-arranged painting, the dummy is dressed in a blue frock coat. His face is a white mask painted with a red bow mouth and red cheeks. Finally, the figure is capped off with a brown wig, complete with pigtail. The mannequin is flying limply through the air, launched from a pinkish blanket held by four well-dressed majas, each highly amused, enjoying themselves, even as their hapless, lifeless subject is "humiliated by four smiling girls, an allusion to women who toy with men's emotions."[76] Too much may be made of the work, but the result is a whimsical, light set piece that anyone with any insight regarding the comings and goings of men and women might ponder.

By December 1791, Goya had completed seven cartoons for tapestries that he billed the factory for that month. Professionally, all was well with the artist. He was much requested for royal and otherwise aristocratic portraits. In a February 1792 letter to Zapater, he mentions his intent to have a genealogy of his family drawn up, likely as a first step to having himself declared a nobleman. In the letter, he described himself with a flattering reference to his importance as "giant Goya."[77] To show how serious he was about becoming aristocracy, he told Zapater he was no longer going to listen to popular, common songs, called seguidillas, since it was important for him to "maintain the dignity that a man should always possess."[78] Goya was definitely riding a wave.

7

A Disturbing
Turn of Events

Events in France were also riding a wave of their own. In 1789, the French people turned on their monarch, having marched on his palace at Versailles. They rounded up Louis XVI, Queen Marie Antoinette, and their son, the Dauphain, and removed them to Paris, the true center of the great upheaval. There, revolutionary leaders could keep an eye on the royal family.

By 1791, the king and queen made a break for safety, escaping from their captivity at the old Parisian palace of the Tuileries. Under cover of darkness, they headed toward the border, but their large, lumbering carriage was spotted and detained just short of the French frontier at the town of Varennes. The king and his family were returned to Paris and the revolution continued, with the question of the future of the monarchy on everyone's mind.

A FEARFUL FUTURE

In Spain, the revolution petrified every nobleman and noble-woman. Anything that even hinted of French liberalism, of Enlightened social theory, or a challenge to royal authority was questioned. By February 1792, the liberal-minded Prime Minister Floridablanca was dismissed from his service to the state and replaced by the aging count of Aranda, who had served Carlos III nearly 20 years earlier and himself had promoted an Enlightened Spain. Aranda was removed within 10 months, only to be replaced by the queen's lover, the 25-year-old Godoy. Godoy was a virile, blond guardsman whom the queen had already promoted in just a few years to lieutenant general of the army, duke of Alcudia, and member of the Council of State. Yet Godoy was incapable of altering the unfolding and disconcerting state of affairs in France. He could do nothing to save the French royal family, fellow Bourbons and cousins to Carlos IV. By August 1792, the French monarchy was dethroned, and by January of the following year, Louis XVI was taken to the scaffold and guillotined. When Spain protested and hinted it would not tolerate the actions being taken by the French revolutionaries, leaders of the new French republic chose to declare war on Spain. The next 20 years would be dark and difficult.

Goya's life was also taking disturbing turns. Little is known of his comings and goings in 1792. There are no known letters in existence today written during that year. It is not even clear how he fell so dramatically out of favor, losing his status as a respected painter to the court, only to become "a virtual outcast."[79] Then, in January 1793, Goya wrote a letter to the accountant of the duke and duchess of Osuna. In it, the artist explains that he has been bedridden for two months. He has been dizzy and has experienced some partial paralysis. What was the disease or condition Goya was suffering from? At the time, the rumor was that Goya had contracted a sexually transmitted disease. That proved not to be the case,

Goya's 1795 portrait of his friend, the duchess of Alba, is recognized as one of his most famous paintings. Goya concentrates his color palette to the repeating dual themes of red and white, with the only other prominent color in the portrait being the subject's long mane of black hair. The duchess was the subject of numerous works by Goya.

however. Doctors today believe he may have been suffering from the effects of some type of meningitis. He might have been experiencing a condition that inflames the nerves of the inner ear. His illness might also have been brought on by Vogt-Koyanagi-Harada syndrome, a rare form of eye disease. One of its symptoms is hearing loss. Whatever Goya had contracted, it was quite bothersome and alarming. In a letter from Zapater to Sebastian Martinez, an art dealer, Goya's friend notes, "As the illness is of the most fearsome nature, it makes me melancholy thinking of his recuperation."[80] (Goya had painted a pensive portrait of Martinez in 1792.)

The illness lasted for most of a year, and for most of that time, Goya was nearly paralyzed. Through those months, Goya was almost in constant pain and chronically tired. In addition, he was losing his hearing. He feared he might go blind, which would have brought his art career to a sad and abrupt end. By February 1794, his old friend Jovellanos noted in his diary that Goya had not even been able to write a response due to his "apoplexy." A later writer would starkly note, "One of the charming artists of the 18th Century was expiring."[81] Death, however, was not the disease's consequence. In time, the paralysis passed. Goya did not become blind. Yet one symptom remained. For the rest of his life, more than 30 years, Francisco Goya was totally deaf. The only sounds he was conscious of "were frightful, unearthly buzzings capable of driving him close to madness."[82]

A SOUNDLESS WORLD

What was Goya to do with this change in his physical abilities? Goya did the only thing he could do: he simply continued working, choosing to ignore his new condition. Even by summer 1793, he found the occasional energy to paint and travel, including attending a meeting of the Royal Academy of San Fernando in Madrid. That summer he began painting a series of 11 small paintings, which he referred to as "cabinet pictures," selecting subject matter that generally "find no place in commissioned works."[83] He painted them just as a distraction from his illness and its accompanying pain. They were small, approximately 16 by 12 inches (40cm by 30cm), painted on tin-coated iron sheets.

When they were shown to the Academy, the members were excited, "celebrating their merit and that of Goya."[84] They were, indeed, subjects off the beaten path. Although not all the paintings are known, it appears they may have included "people fleeing from a fire at night, the survivors of a shipwreck struggling to shore, and, recapitulating his big decorative panel for the Osunas, the holdup of a coach by robbers."[85] Another painting probably portrayed life inside a Spanish prison and another, referred to in the academy's minutes of January 5, 1794, portrayed the inmates in an insane asylum being whipped by their guard. Goya would later say that the *Madhouse* picture depicted "a corral of madmen and two who are fighting, nude, with their keeper beating them and others with sacks (a subject which I witnessed in Saragossa)."[86] All the other paintings appear to have been bullfight pictures.

With war raging between France and Spain, it is not surprising that Goya would receive a pair of commissions in 1793 to paint military portraits. One was of a Spanish general, Antonio Ricardos, who lost his life fighting the following year, and Lieutenant Colonel Felix Colon de Larreategui, whose family had connections with Cabarrus. Another portrait was done of Ramon Posado y Soto, a relative of Jovellanos's brother-in-law. In a letter, the subject mentions that Goya is totally deaf.

REVOLUTIONARY CHANGE

The following year, the French Revolution took a decided turn, one that allowed the Spanish court to breathe a sigh of relief. After experiencing nightmare months of the Reign of Terror, during which thousands of French subjects were killed, counterrevolutionaries had finally turned on the revolution and its excesses. In mid-summer 1794, the revolution's leader,

Maximilien Robespierre, was arrested, hastily tried and convicted, and then guillotined. For the moment, the terror of the French Revolution was over. This change in events helped alleviate some of the political tension that had gripped Madrid for years. One of the benefactors of the change was Goya. New commissions came to him, including those from new patrons, many of whom were friends of earlier supporters of Goya's art. One of Jovellanos's associates, the count of El Carpio (a director of the National Bank of San Carlos), offered Goya a commission to paint his younger wife, the marquise de la Solana.

The painting stands as a tribute to the benevolence and kindness of the 33-year-old marquise. She was known for her charities, especially an orphanage she supported. It is a simple work of an apparently simple woman. She is not an extraordinary beauty: the nose is too large and the eyes too far apart. Yet her face has a kindness about it. The portrait was painted full-length, the painting's lower half presenting a featureless black skirt and petticoats. Her head is framed with a white lace shawl topped by an overly large peach-colored bow that immediately draws the attention of the viewer. Even then, one returns to the soft eyes of the marquise. Goya has captured not only his subject's otherwise unremarkable features, but he has produced a work that reveals her generous heart and selfless support of the unfortunate. Soon after the painting was completed, the marquise died. If Goya had known his subject was terminal, he may have been even more inspired to make it clear that he admired the marquise for her spirited courage.

By 1795, the war between the French and Spanish was over. That summer, the two warring powers, along with Prussia, signed the Treaty of Basel. During the following months, the skies opened up for Goya's formerly suspect friends: Floridablanca was absolved of all accusations, Jovellanos was pardoned, and Cabarrus, after years of imprisonment, was freed. (Amazingly, the queen's favorite, Prime Minister Godoy, received the title of Prince of the Peace.) Goya benefited from this turn in the fortunes of his old friends. He was soon asked to paint one of his most famous paintings, a portrait of the duchess of Alba.

THE DUCHESS OF ALBA

The duchess was, perhaps, one of the most beautiful and alluring women in all of Spain. Nearly every man who had ever met her thought so, and some actually wrote poetry about her beauty. She was slender, with a small waist and taller than many women of her day. Her facial features were alluring, with high cheek bones, dark eyes, and a slip of a bow for a mouth.

WERE THE DUCHESS OF ALBA AND GOYA LOVERS?

During Goya's lifetime and even through the centuries since, rumors abounded that the artist and his most beautiful of subjects became romantically involved with one another. Were the rumors true?

It is known that when Goya painted his first portrait of the duchess of Alba, they may have met in earlier years. There is a story that Goya included her in a couple of his earlier tapestry cartoons. Even so, his playful inclusion of this Spanish beauty does not automatically translate in the two being lovers.

How likely was such a relationship anyway? The duchess was flirty, and affairs appear to have been normal for her. Her husband, the duke, was not known as a virile man, as may be noted in the portrait Goya painted of him. He appears thin, shy, and sensitive, "the antithesis of the ideal Spanish male."[*] It is no wonder that so many men thought they might have had a chance for a relationship with the duchess. Yet what of Goya, who was almost 50 years old and deaf when he painted her first portrait? That Goya might have become infatuated with the duchess is entirely possible. Also, she might have been flattered by having the most celebrated painter in Spain rendering her portrait. Yet the record is silent.

Her heavy eyebrows were made less pronounced by her hair, a massive collection of thick, dark tresses that framed her light skin. (There is an Indian ink wash done by Goya in 1797 titled *The Duchess of Alba Arranging Her Hair*.) A French admirer noted: "The Duchess of Alba has not a hair on her head that does not provoke desire. When she passes everyone looks from their windows and even children leave their games to look at her."[87] She was graceful, a wonderful dancer, with a taste for the seguidillas (the common, earthy songs that Goya says he renounced) and fandangos, the animated, sometimes sweaty

Complicating the question is the death of the duke not long after the duchess's portrait was completed. Following his death, Goya visited the duchess in Sanlucar de Barrameda. While there, from May to July 1796, he was busy with official commissions. Goya also drew sketches in what is known today as the *Sanlucar Notebook*. His sketches include two or three of the duchess. He painted another wonderful portrait of her in 1797. While the earlier portrait became known popularly as the "White Duchess," Goya's 1797 portrait would be called the "Black Duchess," since she was attired in a black mourning dress due to her husband's death. All this—the additional portrait and sketches and the shared experiences—probably means little more than that these two were simply friends: "There is no good reason to suppose that the beauty was ever in bed with the deaf genius twice her age."**

The duchess would not live long after her husband died. She died of tuberculosis at the age of 40.

  * Quoted in Richard Schickel, *The World of Goya, 1746–1828* (New York: Time-Life Books, 1968), 100.
 ** Quoted in Robert Hughes, *Goya* (New York: Alfred A. Knopf, 2003), 159.

dance that would bridge popularity from the eighteenth to the nineteenth centuries. Despite being a member of Spain's aristocratic class, the duchess loved to dress in the costume of a maja, which might provide a context for her more spirited nature. She had many love affairs, yet for all her physical and unrestrained qualities and attributes that men seemed to find so appealing, she may have been an airhead. Yet she was a beautiful and wealthy airhead, whose "wealth was immeasurable—seventeen palaces or mansions and such tracts of land that people thought she could walk the length of Spain without stepping off her estates."[88]

Goya's painting of the duchess of Alba in 1795 (there would be others later) presents her from head to toe, a full-length presentation of her exquisite beauty. She is dressed in a full-length white gown with dashes of vermillion, complemented by a wide waist sash, bows at her bosom and in her hair, and a two-strand necklace of red baubles. Except for the strong bits of red color, the duchess blends well against a backdrop of greenish-yellow mountains and a sea-green sky. Her dress almost disappears into the same-colored, sandy landscape of the painting's bottom half. (The backgrounds Goya included in this painting are significant, since this may be the artist's "first time to place his model in an actual landscape."[89] She is tall and beautiful, yet aloof.

WAR AGAIN FOR SPAIN

Although Godoy was credited with getting Spain through its war with France by 1795, the following year brought a renewal of conflict and of allies. With England still at war with France, the Spanish monarchy was compelled to join with the French against the British by autumn 1796. Godoy's star was growing dimmer. The queen, tired of Godoy's outside female interests, forced him to marry a cousin of Carlos IV. Godoy soon sought the support of such liberals as Cabarrus, which resulted in the appointment of Jovellanos as the minister of justice. Other old friends of Goya's gained influential government appointments, including the new ministers of agriculture and finance. Goya would paint them. His rendering of Jovellanos was of a man who was "elegant, distinguished, a dreamer weighed down by cares, a hint of benevolence in his eyes."[90] Further pressures, mostly from a domineering France, came to bear on Godoy, who was forced to resign his post.

By spring 1798, Goya received a commission from the Queen Maria Luisa to provide paintings for the royal chapel of San Antonio de la Florida. Since the 1600s, the small shrine of San Antonio (St. Anthony) was situated on the ground of la Florida, next to the park of the royal palace. Carlos IV and Maria Luisa purchased the land and replaced the old shrine with a new chapel, San Antonio de la Florida. In decorating the chapel, a 52-year-old, deaf Goya had scaffolding erected so he could paint the chapel's dome. He spent four months on the project, from August through November. It would be a masterpiece of modern art.

A NEW FRESCO

The painting on the dome was titled *The Miracle of San Antonio of Padua*. Goya based his work on a legend from the life of St. Anthony. In the story, the future saint receives word that his Portuguese father has been falsely accused of murdering a man in Lisbon. Instantly, Anthony is transported to Lisbon and requests the magistrate to present him with the murder victim's body. Then he unflinchingly asks the corpse to rise up and testify whether his father was the murderer. To the court's surprise, the dead victim does just that, informing the astonished judges that Anthony's father was innocent. Then the body falls back in its coffin, once again dead as dead can be.

This dramatic scene was translated even more dramatically by Goya's composition, which had to fit into a large round dome. His idea was not new. He chose to paint a false balcony balustrade around the entire dome base with more than four dozen people standing behind it, witnessing the great miracle of St. Anthony. The same technique had been done in Italy

This detail from Goya's *The Miracle of San Antonio of Padua*, shows St. Anthony preaching to an attentive crowd. The painting adorns the dome of the chapel of San Antonio de la Florida in Madrid. Note the simple wooden railing created by Goya as a false balcony for the composition.

long ago. Perhaps Goya had seen examples of it during his youthful Italian sojourn. Yet Goya constructed the painting to make it uniquely his. Instead of a heavy marble balustrade, though, Goya painted a simple ring railing of wood with iron posts. The setting is outdoors, featuring blue mountains, a few trees and a pale, whitish sky. Goya has placed his witnesses all around the false barrier of painted wood and iron, with St. Anthony standing higher than all of them, a miracle worker to be seen.

Yet, each of the assembled respond uniquely to the miracle. Some do not seem surprised at all. Children at play, scrambling for the railing, miss it completely. Others look over the balcony to the church floor below, leaving visitors to watch the people in the fresco watching them. Color is everywhere because the painting is populated with common people, their clothing featuring street splashes of mauves, browns, and deep blues. All this is set against skirts, shawls, and cloaks of white, jade, and hot orange. The sky is gray and leaden, but the people are fit for a miracle or even a bullfight. Goya's crowd is tough, but the composition sings of holiness dispensing justice. All this is done with brushstrokes any nineteenth-century impressionist painter would be proud of. With the dome rising 30 feet (9.1m) above the floor, Goya saw no need to put fine detail on figures that would be lost in the visual distance from floor to ceiling. So,

> . . . a slash of black paint with a blob on the end defines an eyelid and a pupil; another lash, the shadow under a cheekbone or a mouth. . . . The closer you look, the more modern the frescoes get. Once again one sees why Goya's accumulated meaning for painters could only increase as the nineteenth century moved toward the twentieth.[91]

With the dome covered in the miracle scene, Goya was left to decorate the church's nooks and crannies, panels, and arches. Goya turns things upside down by filling these spaces with angels who are below the dome, rather than hovering above it, as angels typically did in other church art. Goya's angels are gorgeous, modern, and sensual. Angels previously were usually painted as sweet choirboys, but Goya chose to paint them as down-to-earth feminine angels dressed in the rich silks and gauzy muslins Spanish girls wore at the end of the eighteenth century. They are pretty things, with their eyes bright, fair skins, and ruby lips. They are hardly stylized heavenly beings. They are more like attractive girls suited up in drapes of richly colored fabrics. One modern critic, emphasizing a comparison between the frescoes' subject matter to that of the later nineteenth-century impressionists, noted how the "angels on the pendentives [dome supports] seem to have emerged from the studio of Auguste Renoir, so far are they in advance of their time."[92]

8

Rising Star, Dark Shadows

These were extraordinarily productive days for Goya. Not only did he work on the San Antonio frescoes and several commissioned portraits, but he also completed a work titled *The Betrayal of Christ* for the Cathedral of Toledo. Within just a few months of the completion of the frescoes at San Antonio de la Florida, Goya announced the publication of a collection of etched prints he had been working on for several years. It was a group of approximately 80 startling, disturbing etchings that Goya titled as *Caprichos (The Caprices)*. The works were mostly done following the prolonged illness that had delivered Goya near death's door, only to leave him physically crushed and totally deaf.

THE CAPRICES

The collection of black line etchings went on sale in February 1799. The severe content, however, was not popular and even struck a nerve on the part of late eighteenth-century Spanish society. By order of the Inquisition, the collection was withdrawn from sale after only two days. Goya had sold only 27 copies, including four sets to the duke and duchess of Osuna, his longtime patrons and friends.

Technically, they were wonders of print work. Goya revealed just how much he had mastered the medium of etching works on blank sheets of copy. Yet they were the work of a man nearly mad with illness with a constant ringing in his ears. They are dark works, filled with macabre scenes that torment their victims; satires that reveal the foolishness of man. They were well-intended works, for nearly all were accompanied by a moral or watch phrase meant to warn and inform.

Many people thought that Goya's etchings were too dark, too negative, too cynical, too inflammatory, and too modern. Goya mocked all sorts of social behaviors and institutions—prostitution, superstition, vices and vanities, and even the Inquisition. His critics claimed that the etchings would frighten the weak minded: there are dreams filled with winged monsters, naked witches fly through the air on broomsticks, an angry horse bites a woman. There is an unhappily married couple tied together, literally struggling to be free. There are hobgoblins, apparitions, phantoms, and a hanged man. All is dark, folly traps Goya's subjects, and the stupid are everywhere and always with us: it is the way of the world.

Goya cautions his viewers not only through his etchings but through the captions that accompany them, just in case the symbolism of a winged young lady in the clutches of a pair of lecherous men was not clear enough: "The sleep of reason produces monsters." "The world is a masquerade. Face, dress and voice, all are false." "She who wants to be caught never escapes." "He who does not like you will defame you in jest." "Negligence, tolerance and spoiling make children capricious, naughty, vain, greedy, lazy and insufferable." Goya added to this collection in later years. These works were known as the *Disparates (Follies)* and *Proverbios (Proverbs)*. They created equally chilling scenes of the grotesque and disturbing, along with the same aphorisms: "Renounce the friend who covers you with his wings and bites you with his beak." "She who is ill-wed never misses a chance to say so." This type of content was not acceptable in the religiously conservative environment of late eighteenth-century Spain.

Although *The Caprices* caused enough of a swirl of controversy to have the Spanish Inquisition inform the artist that he would have to withdraw the sale of his etchings from the public market, Goya does not seem to have taken any significant career hits as an artist. In fact, in September 1799, the most important political force in Spain, Queen Maria Luisa, contacted Goya and commissioned him to paint her portrait. He had painted both the king and queen 10 years earlier. The painting very much pleased her, and led her to ask the Aragonese artist to paint her again, this time as if riding on horseback. (The work was done in the studio, rather than outdoors with a live horse.) There the queen sits, an aging, relatively unattractive woman but regally dressed in conservative black, festooned with slashes of red and gold. She almost appears like a man: booted foot in the stirrup, firm hand at the reins, and wearing a wide-brimmed black hat and a look of assurance. She liked the second portrait even more than Goya's first. "It's said to be a better likeness than the portrait in the mantilla," she wrote to Goya in a letter.[93] (Perhaps not to be outdone, Carlos IV ordered a similar, complimentary portrait of himself done, also on horseback, his chest brimming with royal sashes and medals.) Goya could not have been happier. In yet another letter to Zapater, he wrote, "The royals are mad about me."[94]

AT HIS ZENITH
Goya was on the verge of the apogee, or highest point, of his career. The years from 1799 to 1808 were years of stunning accomplishment and success. In October 1799, he was given the position of First Court Painter, a position for which he

In 1800, Goya painted his most important portrait, *Family of Carlos IV*, in which he seemingly mocks the royal family. The king, decked out in gaudy medals, appears as a piggish man, and his wife, Queen Maria Luisa, standing with the children, looks unattractive and unintelligent. Goya is in the far left background, appearing as the objective chronicler of the arrogance of this failed Spanish monarch.

had longed for many years. His salary was set at 50,000 reales annually, plus a carriage. Over the two years that followed, he painted, possibly, his most important and greatest portrait, the *Family of Carlos IV*.

Yet even as Goya's star was rising in Spain, someone else's star was also finding a new place on the European horizon. In November 1799, the legendary French general, Napoleon Bonaparte, having triumphantly returned from campaigns of conquest in Italy and Egypt, overthrew the postrevolutionary government, the Directory. Napoleon wasted no time in challenging the powers of Europe, several of whom went to war against him, including Great Britain and Austria. With already existing ties between the French and Spain, the Spanish monarchy officially fell into line and agreed to Napoleon's control. The new French dictator soon placed Godoy once again in power in Madrid. Several of the liberals in Spain, the ilustados, including Cabarrus, found themselves losing their influence. Some were even exiled.

As for Goya, he managed to deftly steer clear of the shifting politics that might have ensnared someone else. He did not align himself with anyone who might cost him his position or influence. Goya was never a particularly political creature, so hitching his wagon to one political star over another made little sense other than how it might directly affect him. With all the political changes happening to those around him, Goya found himself busy house hunting by January 1800. His motivation for moving was that the house he had occupied since 1778 was bought out from under him by the returning Godoy for his mistress, Pepita Tudo. Six months later, Goya purchased the property at 15 Calle Valverde, near the Calle del Desengano. It would be the first house that Goya ever owned.

That spring, Goya painted a portrait of the wife of the man who was forcing him out of his home. By April 1800, the artist was at work painting the portrait of Godoy's wife, the countess of Chinchon, whom Queen Maria Luisa had forced him to marry years earlier. The painting became one of Goya's best female portraits, rivaling the portrait of the marquise de la Solana. The painting, unlike most of his portraits of this period, was not set outdoors but rather in the

(continues on page 106)

"A MAN OF GENIUS"

Today, with almost two centuries having passed between the death of Francisco Goya and the birth of modern art, the artist is considered one of the greatest painters of Western culture and civilization. This is actually a relatively new phenomenon, for, even though he is admired as a painter of great genius today, many of his works were generally either unknown or inaccessible for decades following his death. Many of his paintings were held in "royal apartments or private collections that could be entered only with the proper introductions."[*]

The works that would provide the basis for much of his modern fame as an artist—his drawings, the carefully stored cartoons used to create his tapestries, the "black paintings" he created on the walls of his rural house, and his *Caprichos* and *Los Desastres de la Guerra (The Disasters of War)* etchings that hardly saw the light of day—were generally not accessible or even known much outside of Spain. Throughout much of the nineteenth century, a trip to Spain could be an arduous journey, and Goya remained undiscovered.

During the 1800s, even among those who did gain access to Goya's works, his art was not as appreciated for how it would later be seen. Only a small group of artists, including the French painters Delacroix, Daumier, and Manet, really grasped the significance and import of Goya's art. They understood him, because they were, in part, among those artists who would inherit the direction in which Goya took art during his lifetime.

The story for Goya and his artistic legacy is a different one in today's world. He is universally hailed as a modern painter, perhaps even the founder and creator of modern art. His artistic style served as a forerunner to the impressionists and even the expressionists. He came to be seen, as he was seen in his lifetime, as "an artist of surprising talent . . . a man of genius whose exceptional gifts are better understood every day."**

Perhaps one of the most important factors that provides Goya with his legacy of being a modern master, a forerunner of later artistic movements, lies in the longevity of his career. He was an artist who painted and created etchings into his eighties. His artistic life began in one century and ended in another. Those two centuries, the 1700s and 1800s, provide the frameworks for, basically, two art careers, two artistic styles for Goya. If he had died as a young artist in the eighteenth century, he might be remembered today as little more than a second-tier mimic of other artists of his time.

By the nineteenth century, however, Goya's art was changing to fit or even define a new artistic era. His later works are seen today as more expressive, emotional, depicting "a new, realistic look at man and nature."*** War, revolution, the oppressions of absolute monarchs, economic extremes, genocide and other influences of the new century of the 1800s were drawing artists away from the frivolous, away from the pursuit of happiness, and toward a more cynical approach to art. Goya's art became more about tragedy, anxiety, restlessness, destruction, and cynicism.

Perhaps these are the elements of his art works that make him so popular and so understood as a painter today. His later paintings, those expressive, emotional works created in the midst of the swirl of international events, are part of an undeniable artistic legacy that keeps modern art admirers returning to those same works today.

*   Quoted in Claus Virch, *Francisco Goya* (New York: McGraw-Hill Book Company, 1967), 5.

**   Ibid.

***   Ibid., 6.

(continued from page 103)

shrouded darkness of an interior, mysteriously illuminating the subject. The countess is dressed in a silvery muslin gown that shimmers against her seated figure. She is pensive, with a burst of auburn hair escaping her smallish bonnet, along with ears of wheat, a symbol of fertility. The countess, it appears, is pregnant. At the time of the painting, she and Godoy were not speaking, she having become weary of her husband's extramarital affairs. Goya paints her sympathetically and tenderly, yet the countess is aloof, glancing away from the viewer as if her privacy has been violated.

As quietly and shyly as Goya portrayed the countess of Chinchon, he would paint a portrait of Godoy the following year, placing him amid the excitements of the battlefield. Titled *Godoy as Commander in the War of the Oranges*, it depicted a campaign Godoy had fought against Portugal the previous year. There the man who had brazenly loved the queen of Carlos IV sits, amid the rocks, reading a dispatch, flanked by an adjutant on his left and a draped field flag at his right. He is the epitome of the commander.

A NEW MASTERPIECE

By fall 1800, Goya had completed the sketches of the individuals who would be included in his painting of the royal family he had begun the previous year. The resulting painting, *Family of Carlos IV*, is considered a Goya masterpiece. Although the 13 royally-connected figures are surrounded by the darkness that hangs over a room where large paintings dominate the adjacent wall, the entourage seems to sparkle with the accoutrements of royal splendor. They are wearing their best, a spectacular and colorful array of blues, creams, and reds intended to dazzle the viewer with the enviable privilege of rank. Gems, strings of pearls, tiaras, medallions, swords, and golden embroidery illuminate the work.

Yet these baubles and beads only manage to offset the blank looks of nearly everyone in the painting. The queen's face has the appearance of a dough-faced matron who forgot to put in her false teeth. She is a study in contrasts, a 48-year-old woman who "had borne 10 or 12 children, but is wearing a Cupid's dart in her hair in the latest French fashion."[95] As one art historian has noted: "It is remarkable that she accepted Goya's likeness of her."[96] The king stands blankly, looking more like a servant wearing someone else's clothes. The others simply appear alternately haughty, distracted, curious, and even startled, as in the youngest son, the six-year-old Infante Francisco de Paula Antonio, holding the hand of the queen. Despite the glitter and gold of the painting, the queen and king have been so humanized by Goya that they were later described by a French novelist as looking like "the corner baker and his wife after they have won the lottery."[97] The only subjects of the painting who do not appear uncomfortable in his or her own shoes is Goya himself, whose three-quarter profile appears in the dark of the painting's background, and perhaps the young girl at the queen's right side, the angelic Dona Maria Isabel. In clothing and jewelry, she is almost the double of her mother. Yet, her youth reveals an innocence, a softness, and a simpleness that reminds the viewer of Goya's fondness and skill for painting children.

THE NAKED MAJA

At about the time Goya finished his masterful portrait of the royal family late in 1800, he probably completed another painting, a special work for Godoy. It became a matter of controversy and speculation at the time and has remained such over the past two centuries. The painting has been titled, *La Maja desnuda (The Naked Maja)*. It was in Godoy's possession by November 12, 1800, "where it was seen by a visitor in a cabinet dedicated to the female nude."[98] Among the other works in the secret cabinet was a 1650 painting by Velázquez of another reclining, nude woman.

Goya's was a full-length horizontal painting of a young woman who was probably Godoy's mistress, Pepita Tudo, for whom Goya had been forced to move earlier in the year. It was a work destined to become an icon of not only Goya's early nineteenth-century art but of modern art itself. The subject is simple: an unabashed and unashamed young woman lying on a pile of pillows stark naked, her arms lifted coyly above her head and a knowing smile on her face. Such a painting was a gamble at the time for Goya. Generally, depictions of nude women was taboo in Spanish art of that era, an infraction of social mores that would likely draw the attention of the Inquisition. The purpose of the work is clear: to celebrate the physical beauty of a confident woman for whom eroticism might be simply second nature.

There would be additional commissions from Godoy to Goya between 1801 and 1803, including several small paintings to decorate the Spanish leader's palace, as well as a second painting of maja, *La Maja Vestida (Clothed Maja)*. It was a duplicate of the portrait of the naked Pepita, but this time the coy mistress is portrayed wearing clothing. During that time, summer 1802, the duchess of Alba died following a month-long illness (rumor at the time told of her being poisoned by the queen or even Godoy). Goya appears to have been driven to complete a sketch in memory of his friend. Otherwise, there is no record of any other response on the part of the artist to her death.

In 1803, Goya saw the royal family again, but not to paint a portrait. Since selling prints of *The Caprices* had been shut down, Goya chose to sell the original copper plates to Carlos IV and use the money to help his 19-year-old son, Xavier, in his various travels. It would be an important exchange between king and artist, for it would mark the last time Goya would see the monarch until 1808. Through those five years, he continued to be paid as court painter, but did no portraits of the royals. He did continue to work, however, with other commissions and managed to save enough money to purchase another house, this one at Calle de los Reyes in Madrid. It would be the largest, grandest home he would ever own, "a

Painted between 1801 and 1803, *The Clothed Maja* is almost a duplicate of Goya's masterpiece, *The Naked Maja*. It is reported that the original owner of both paintings, Manuel de Godoy, hung *The Clothed Maja* in front of *The Naked Maja* so that *The Naked Maja* could be revealed at any time with a pulley device.

granite-walled affair with a paved porch and courtyard in a fashionable quarter."[99]

One of his important works in 1803 was a portrait, *The Count of Fernan Nuñez*. Art historians have referred to it as the male portrait most similar to Goya's portrait of Godoy's wife, *The Countess of Chinchon*. Stylistically, it is close in quality to the female portrait. The work "like the royal portraits, approaches open satire."[100] It is a full-length picture of the count, dominated by black, including the subject's boots, cloak, cape, tricorn hat, and bushy sideburns. A hand raised to the heart, a gallant right foot forward, a cocked left elbow, and a gaze into the distance as if the count were viewing something important, make the stance appear beyond regal:

the pose is almost comically heroic. (The count, of course, would never hold any real power, having to settle for an assignment at the Spanish embassy in London.) Nevertheless, the portrait of the 24-year-old Nuñez reveals Goya as a completely mature artist "perfectly marrying stylization and realism."[101] Ultimately, it must have been a portrait that pleased, because Nuñez, a member of the Academy of San Fernando, would be one of eight who would vote for Goya to become the new director of the Academy. (Goya would lose that election after another painter, Gregorio Ferro, received 29 votes.)

THE NAKED AND THE CLOTHED MAJA: WHO WAS SHE?

The Naked Maja and *The Clothed Maja* remain a pair of the most intriguing paintings ever done by Goya. They are mirror images of one another, except that in one, the female subject is fully clothed, while in the second, she is naked. In both works, "she is sultry, desirable, seductively immodest."* For Goya's art, she is a milestone, and for the history of Western art, she is an enigma, "one of the most provocative and magnetic figures ever painted."** Yet just exactly who was the beauty?

Some art historians have identified her as the duchess of Alba, with whom Goya allegedly had an affair. Supposedly, the love-crazed artist painted his dual tribute to both the public woman and the private. A better explanation is that she is probably Pepita Tuda, mistress of the Spanish prime minister, Manuel Godoy, who was also a lover to Queen Maria Luisa. This answer springs from the fact that both paintings wound up in the household inventory of Godoy's estate. This, of course, is not irrefutable proof, and the claim that she is the duchess of Alba has never ceased.

During the 1940s, members of the Alba family went to great lengths to disprove the claim. They agreed to allow her grave to

AN ESTABLISHED RHYTHM

Other private commissions remained on Goya's plate during these years, each furthering an already illustrious career. He painted a friend of Cabarrus's, the marquis de San Adrian in 1804, a well-executed work that carries off influences including English portraiture style, which featured the marquis standing with his legs crossed. It is a painting complete with "great attention to accurately rendering and coloring the open, sympathetic expression on the young face."[102] Such works for Goya, now a man in his late fifties, have become second nature to the artist. He is so skilled as a craftsman that it is

be exhumed "to compare the measurements of the skeleton with those of the *maja* in the painting."[***] Yet all those examinations revealed were two broken legs that probably occurred "when her casket was dropped during a French raid on the cemetery at the time of the Napoleonic wars."[†]

Yet how did this painting ever come to be in the first place? In Goya's time, artwork depicting the female nude, especially one as clearly sexualized as this one, were almost nonexistent in Spain. In fact, Goya's painting did get him into trouble. He was called before the Spanish Inquisition in 1814, where he faced a charge of obscenity. Nothing is known of his trial, but he was never jailed, and the painting was never banned, even though it was confiscated. And yet, in the swirl of controversy over one of his most famous paintings, Goya never told anyone who the woman in his artistic masterpiece actually was.

  * Quoted in Richard Schickel, *The World of Goya, 1746–1828* (New York: Time-Life Books, 1968), 68.
 ** Ibid.
*** Ibid.
  † Ibid.

"no longer possible for Goya to paint badly."[103] In later years, Xavier would reflect on his father's talent at this stage of his life, declaring of him, "there was nothing left . . . to conquer in painting . . . he knew the magic [this was a term used constantly by Goya] of atmosphere in a picture."[104] Everything lay at his feet. He was the painter for the royal family and a member of the Academy of San Fernando. He had won nearly all the honors available to a Spanish artist of his time. He was wealthy beyond most people's dreams. Yes, he was deaf and had been for several years, but the driven Goya had surpassed his handicap. He had accepted it a long time ago, and it seemed irrelevant to him.

In this first decade of a new century for Goya, the artist may well have believed that his life was reaching its quiet final years that could easily be filled with more portraits of everything from royalty to street life in Madrid. His son would soon marry. There was a rhythm to Goya's world. He could have easily and reasonably assumed by 1805 that his most important years were already behind him. Yet that assumption, if indeed Goya ever reconciled himself to it, would soon be shattered. International events would change the history of Spain as well as the life of the artist. Godoy, Napoleon, and the Spanish royal family would prove to be the catalyst in these events. This triad would cause a chain of events that would cause Goya to break from what had probably become the artist's predictability, leading him to stretch himself more than he had in years and achieve new heights of influence and artistic success.

9

The Second of May and *The Third of May*

The changes that would bring redirection to Spain and to Goya would begin to take shape by fall 1805. On October 21, in the Mediterranean waters off Cape Trafalgar, located along the southwestern shores of Spain, a tremendous sea battle unfolded. This naval engagement would both crown and crush. Warships of the British fleet, under the command of Lord Horatio Nelson, broke from the usual plan of sailing in a long line parallel to the enemy's vessels and then trying to blast the enemy out of the water. Nelson ordered his ships to sail *into* the enemy, which included ships of both the allied French and Spanish fleets. Nelson won the day, even as he lost his life from a wound he received during the heat of the engagement.

Yet this great naval victory would cause other dominoes to fall. The victory led Napoleon to step up his march. From 1805 to 1807, he consolidated victories over his European enemies, including the Austrians, the Prussians, and the Russians. By 1807, Napoleon had reached the peak of his political power and military might. By the end of the year, in an effort to expand the scope of his empire, French armies occupied Portugal, Spain's neighbor on the Iberian Peninsula. From there, Napoleon launched campaigns in Spain, overthrowing the Spanish monarch, Carlos IV, after 20 years of rule. Napoleon then installed one of his brothers as the new king of Spain.

Despite the establishment of a French monarch in Spain, Spanish resistance did not end. Small bands of guerrilla soldiers continued to harass the French for years. These fighters were ordinary Spaniards, not professional soldiers, and they fought with anything they could—farming tools, axes, wooden sticks, even roofing tiles—keeping the forces of Napoleon tied up for six or seven years. These years of war in Spain, known as the Peninsular War, lasted until 1814.

GOYA'S WORK CONTINUES

During the years directly prior to this protracted war between Spain and France, Goya was busy with his commissioned portraits. The subjects were slightly different, however, from earlier years in that Goya was painting more portraits of men and women who made up Spain's expanding middle class. In 1805, Goya's son, Xavier, turned 21 and got married. The following year, Goya became a grandfather. Goya turned 60 years old, but he was not about to slow down, and, despite his deafness and other physical distractions, he continued to paint. He was wealthy enough to retire, but stopping the work he loved was not a goal. Instead, he was able to rely on his relative wealth to "survive all the political upheavals he witnessed."[105]

These political events caught up with Goya's art in 1808. That year, the French forced Carlos IV to abdicate his throne in favor of his son, who would become Ferdinand VII. Goya was immediately commissioned by the Academy of San Fernando to paint a portrait of the younger king on horseback.

The king managed to find time to pose for Goya, but before the painting was finished, Ferdinand was forced to give up his throne to one of Napoleon's brothers. Goya had to finish the portrait from memory. That spring, the events of May 2 and May 3 took place—two days of terror that Goya would later memorialize in two paintings.

From 1808 to 1814, the years of war between France and Spain would be difficult for Goya. There were divided loyalties among his old friends. Floridablanca and Jovellanos spoke out in favor of a new liberal, nationalist government, while Cabarrus supported Napoleon's brother, Joseph, known as the Intruder King. At first, Goya did not choose sides in the political conflicts that swirled throughout Madrid. Yet by 1810, he came out in favor of the patriots who fought against the French.

During these years of struggle and strife, Goya produced several large paintings that would further his reputation as one of Spain's greatest artists. They included such works as *Majas on a Balcony, Young Women, Time (The Old Women), The Forge,* and *Lazarillo de Tormes.* These paintings are important works for Goya, as they represent a style that was ahead of its time. With the possible exception of *Time,* an allegory portraying the passing of the years, the works are straight-forward scenes from Spanish life, all done in a style that borders on impressionistic. *The Majas on a Balcony* was a tease, featuring two young, attractive women wearing the gowns, draperies, and lace of the majas. As they sit on a balcony, they watch passersby. Perhaps they are prostitutes, but they are made more brazen and mysterious by the two black-shrouded male figures who stand behind them. Here, Goya has created the majas' "sparkling embroidery" on their clothing "with pigment applied by rapid thrusts of the palette knife which contrasts with other parts of delicate transparency."[106] Of these paintings, perhaps *Young Women* and *The Forge* reflect the future of Western art the clearest. The colors in both are based on muted tones surrounded by shades of gray, thrown on their canvases with bold brushstrokes. Nineteenth-century impressionism appears just around the corner. With such works, Goya is painting, not from commission, but choosing subjects that strike his fancy, revealing the artistic liberty he has come to enjoy.

Despite such freedom, Goya never puts at arm's length the war his countrymen were experiencing with the French. He takes on the subject and produces several stark, even shocking paintings. Two such works were produced between 1808 and 1810, *Brigands Stripping a Woman* and *Brigands Shooting Their Prisoners*. The works are done in muted shades, all dark

NAPOLEON: THE NEMESIS TO THE NORTH

During much of the quarter century from 1789 to 1814, Spain was at war with France. During the 1790s, the war was first spurred by the execution of the French monarch, Louis XVI. The Bourbons had been removed from power. This led to a coalition of nations, including England, the Netherlands, and Spain, to join with Austria and Prussia, two nations already at war with France. This War of the First Coalition ended successfully for the revolutionary government of France in 1797, after it defeated all of France's enemies except England.

By 1798, the War of the Second Coalition opened with France facing England, Russia, Austria, and Turkey. By the following year, Napoleon claimed power for himself in France, ultimately declaring himself emperor in 1804. By 1801, the second war was successfully won, this time by Napoleon. Yet war was not over. England continued to struggle against the French, and in 1805, the War of the Third Coalition began, with Austria and Russia joining England again.

From 1805 to 1808, Napoleon appeared invincible on the battlefield. He invaded the German states in the fall of 1805, where he defeated an Austrian army. He defeated the Austrians and stark. They are intended to portray the horrors of war and its consequences. While their messages are clear, they are most notable because of Goya's mastery of creating works that balance the qualities of light and shade.

They are reminiscent of Rembrandt at his best: darkness interrupted by thin golden light, the humans so natural and stripped of fancy that their presence on the canvases may be actually felt. Goya painted additional war-themed canvases, such as *Making Gunpowder in the Sierra Tardienta* and *Making Bullets*. In 1810, he also produced a series of etchings designed to portray death and destruction. The series was titled *The*

again two months later. The following year, Napoleon organized the Confederation of the Rhine, an alliance of German states including Saxony, Bavaria, and Wurttemberg against the Prussians and the Austrians. Napoleon then defeated the Russians and the Prussians and negotiated a treaty ending their involvement in the war.

The French emperor would subsequently invade the Iberian Peninsula, first to fight the Portuguese, then overthrowing the Spanish monarch in 1808. Yet the Spanish people would not surrender to Napoleon, and they waged a guerrilla campaign known as the Peninsular War that stretched on from 1808 to 1814. This fierce resistance against the French would be crucial to the ultimate fate of Napoleon. Through those years, it helped bottle up perhaps as many as 250,000 French troops on the Iberian Peninsula, forces Napoleon could not use on other battlefields.

Ultimately, Napoleon overextended himself when he invaded Russia in 1812, losing his Grande Armée of 600,000 men. By spring 1813, a new coalition of European powers was closing in on the French dictator. Napoleon was finally defeated in 1814, drawing the eight-year conflict in Spain to a close.

Disasters of War, which focuses repeatedly on such scenes as piles of corpses. They are atrocity pictures, never intended for publication. The first public printing would not take place until 1863, nearly 50 years later, decades after Goya's death. Of the roughly 80 prints, about 20 percent of them show the gruesome effects of starvation in Madrid during the years 1811 to 1812. Among the starkest is an etching of a newly deceased, young mother being carried to her grave by three somber men as her toddler child weeps.

ACCELERATED EVENTS

By 1812, events were moving quickly. For Goya, the most immediate and personal was the death of his wife, Josefa, at age 65, in June. Her death required a legal listing of her property, which gives historians a view of Goya's finances. It appears that Goya's net worth stood at 360,000 reales. Yet other, more political, events would bring further change to Goya's life. The war with France would eventually end. Napoleon's forces in Russia were facing ruin in 1812. The following year brought further defeat for the French, this time on the Iberian Peninsula at the hands of the English military officer, Arthur Wellesley, who would later become known by his title, the Duke of Wellington. Goya would witness the transfer of power back to Ferdinand VII, who made his triumphal return to Madrid by May of 1814. (Through such changes in power, Goya managed to keep his place as court painter through the reign of Joseph Bonaparte, just as he had served Carlos IV. He would continue as the royal painter for Ferdinand.)

The return of Ferdinand received mixed responses. The Spanish king quickly destroyed the new, liberal constitution that had been voted on by the Spanish Parliament in 1812. The parliament had been operating in exile in the city of Cádiz, in southwestern Spain. Although history judges Ferdinand harshly for the move, the Spanish public gave him their support. To them, "he was seen as the saviour who had overthrown the Napoleonic Antichrist."[107] Ferdinand, with his

Goya's tribute to the citizens of Madrid, *The Second of May, 1808*, captures the early moments of the crowd's uprising against the Mamelukes of the French Imperial Guard. Goya portrays his fellow countrymen as heroes, using crude weapons against a well-trained, professional army. The scene purposely lacks a single focus point: Goya's intention is to show the chaotic nature of what actually happened that day.

conservative intentions, chose to abandon all liberal reforms in Spain and restore power to his throne and to the Catholic Church. For many, these moves were viewed as returning to better days. Despite the changes, however, Goya remained court painter.

Goya recorded the French response to the uprisings of May 2, 1808, in *The Third of May, 1808*. This scene shows the murders on Principe Pio hill, one of several places where Spanish citizens were shot. The central figure, dressed in a white shirt as a symbol of innocence, looms above his fallen friends, staring bravely at the faceless enemy.

During these political changes, Goya painted political subjects. With the French gone, the aging Aragonese artist painted the *Allegory of the Constitution of 1812*, which revealed his allegiance to liberal politics that supported a written framework of government at the expense of the unlimited power of a monarch. The painting is a pink and blue tribute to liberalism in Spain. Yet the constitution Goya praised in paint would soon be scrapped by the autocratic Ferdinand. Next, Goya made an official request from the returning Spanish monarch "to commemorate with my paintbrush the most notable and heroic actions of our glorious rebellion against the tyrant of Europe."[108] He was referring, of course, to the events of nearly six years earlier on May 2 and May 3, 1808: the bloody, spontaneous uprising in the streets of Madrid against the removal of the Spanish royal family and the French reprisals that followed the next day. Ferdinand gave his permission.

A PAIR OF PAINTINGS

Goya's paintings would become iconic symbols of French brutality against the Spanish people and would serve as two of Spain's greatest propaganda paintings. (In the late 1930s, Pablo Picasso's monochromatic painting, *Guernica*, a response to Fascist atrocities in Spain, also served as a powerful piece of Spanish propaganda art.) Goya would not set his two works in a typical military setting of two European armies clashing across a chaotic battlefield of war. Instead, his paintings focus on the heroism of the average, street-level Spanish civilian who rose up voluntarily and suddenly against the French. The paintings are intimate, set close in on the violence.

In *The Second of May, 1808,* Goya crowds his canvas with two dozen subjects clashing in the streets of Madrid. Everything is arranged so tightly that the viewer's eyes move from person to person so naturally that the entire work seems to move on its own. The scene is frantic, frenzied, and kinetic, as motion and emotion dominate. Nothing is subtlety portrayed. The anger, fear, and rage seen on the faces of the Spanish rioters can almost be touched or felt. These emotions are embodied most significantly in the wild-eyed look of the assassin standing at the painting's center: his

dagger is raised to slash in anger at a Mameluke who has
already been dealt a deathblow and is falling upside down
and off his white charger. Other daggers are raised with equal

FRIENDS AND CONFIDANTS

Through entire phases of his life, Francisco Goya could be considered
a solitary man. He was not always prone to strong, emotional friendships, and sometimes he seems so busy with his career that he had
few close friends. Yet friendship was an important aspect of Goya's
personality, even if friends seem to have come and gone sometimes
with regularity.

Among Goya's friends, none towers greater than the young man he
met at school, a fellow student at the Escuela Pia who would continue
as his comrade for decades to follow—Martin Zapater. So much of
what is known about the personable Goya is known through the many
letters that the Spanish artist wrote over the years to his friend and
confidant. Although the two met on common ground as young men,
Zapater remained a close and essential comrade in the life of the adult
Goya, even after his friend became famous and associated with kings.

Although they did not always live in close proximity to one another
in later decades, Zapater served as a good anchor for Goya. They were
not alike in every way, and Zapater was able to understand those differences and help his friend through difficult times, including depres-
sions. It is important to understand that, although Goya became
famous and successful and Zapater less so, the artist continued to turn
to the friend of his youth as a sounding board and for moral support.

While Zapater was a constant friend in the long life of Goya, others came along at various points during his career. Among those with
the greatest influences were three who would have dramatic impacts
on the history of Spain during Goya's lifetime. They included the
count of Floridablanca, Pedro de Campomanes, and Gaspar Melchor
de Jovellanos. Of the three, Floridablanca and Campomanes would

fervor by combatants on both sides. All is chaos and clamor as French soldiers fall. The spirits of the Spanish rise as the rioters seize the opportunity they have gained to take their revenge

have the most significant influences on the life of the Spanish artist. They were open-minded men whose enlightened outlooks meshed well with that of Goya's worldly, sometimes even cynical, view of humanity. These two were involved in the business world and in politics, and Goya learned from them and was helped by their personal and professional careers. It was Floridablanca, after all, who, as Spanish royal minister, probably introduced Goya to King Carlos's brother, the Infante, Don Luis de Bourbon, who became an important patron of Goya's.

It was also Floridablanca who introduced Goya to the duke and duchess of Osuna, who became not only patrons of the artist, but friends as well. For 30 years, the duke and duchess (Goya first knew them as the marquis and marquise de Penafiel) were great supporters. The artist would be the duchess's favorite painter. Between the works he created through their support, Goya would become known as the best portrait artist in Spain.

Among his circle of important and influential friends, Goya also counted other aristocratic women. The duchess of Alba, one of the most beautiful women in Spain, became a friend, confidant, and patron. Some even hinted that Goya and the duchess might have been lovers, but there was a 17-year difference in their ages, and no evidence of a sexual relationship exists.

In the end, what about those whom Goya considered among his circle of friends? Did they include fellow artists, those who may have shared artistic tendencies with the Spanish artist? While he did have artistic influences and short-lived painter friendships, it appears that Goya's friends were typically those who were among his patrons and supporters, rather than his fellow artists.

on their invaders. The arrangement is classically painted, one that could have been of a Roman or Greek battle scene. Yet Goya has brought new emotion to the action, which is both pedestrian and noble.

With his second painting, Goya creates a totally different work. While the *Second of May, 1808* is a crowded and confused scene with strong political, liberal, and secular overtones, "the *Third of May* has more of a character of a religious altarpiece—dedicated, however, to the religion of patriotism."[109] Just as the main character in his *Second of May* composition is a black-haired, mustachioed man who sports thick black sideburns, so the focal point of his *Third of May* painting is a similar individual. Could he be the same man in both paintings? Is the murderer of Mamelukes now the agonized victim of a French firing squad? It is an intriguing question, but the answer is unknown.

Regardless, the *Third of May* presents a disturbing image of anguish as Spanish men are lined up and shot. The painting has a modern look and feel, with its impressionistic brushstrokes and its heavy reliance on violence and emotion. It is a painting not only painted to *look* outdoors, as many studio paintings were, it appears it was *painted* outdoors. There are the French, on their brutal outdoor stage, as automaton soldiers, their anonymous faces turned away from the viewer, preparing to gun down the Spanish insurgents. All is dark, except for a large box lantern that illuminates the soldiers' human targets and brilliantly emphasizes the dark-haired man, dressed in a stark white peasant shirt and muted yellow pants.

The painting also appears modern through its subject matter, as if it were a journalist's snapshot of an event worth remembering. There is an immediacy and personality to the painting, as if Goya had actually been there as a witness of French retaliation. It is all thrown in the viewer's face, with a no-holds-barred realism. It is brutal and direct, with "no rhetoric, no contrived symbolism, no traditional pictorial formula, no stale studio atmosphere."[110] This painting will come to symbolize the new art of the early nineteenth century, born in a world where change was demanded, where liberalism was bound to replace absolutism, and where the Enlightenment was to be challenged by not another political revolt but a revolution formed around feeling something. It would be called the Romantic Rebellion—and Goya would be one of its founders.

10

House of the Deaf Man

The war might have been over, but Spain was in a catastrophic state. Spaniards, including Goya, soon understood they had merely changed a foreign dictator, Joseph Bonaparte, for a domestic one, Ferdinand VII. Ferdinand gathered all power around him, persecuting Spanish liberals and those who had been loyal to France, the *afrancesados* (the Frenchified). (Some of Goya's more controversial, political canvases had to be hidden from royal eyes in the Academy of San Fernando. They would remain there until Ferdinand's death in 1833.) Anyone who might have aided or cooperated with the French was considered suspect. Even though Goya was "cleared of all suspicion of collaboration,"[111] Ferdinand did not trust him. Yet he allowed the great painter to continue to paint. It was at this time that Goya painted a famous work, *Portrait of General Don Jose de Palafox on Horseback.*

THE AGING ARTIST

Although Goya was approaching 70 years, he had lost none of his spark for life and its possibilities. A self-portrait, painted in 1815, reveals a Goya who is still vibrant, feisty, and painting as boldly as ever. After 1815, he was painting fewer and fewer works in the Spanish court, just an occasional portrait. He painted everything by choice, including a series of bullfighting pictures. He seemed untouchable, as if no one could change or control him. By 1816, his etchings, *The Caprices*, were put back on sale to the public. Goya had worked long enough as a painter by then that he found himself painting portraits of the children of earlier subjects, such as the son and daughter of the duke and duchess of Osuna. He also painted pictures of saints for the Cathedral of Seville.

By 1819, he moved to a country villa, across the Manzanares River from Madrid, near the meadow of San Isidro, which he had memorialized in paint years earlier. (The house next door to Goya's was known as, ironically, the Quinta del Sordo, or House of the Deaf Man. After his death, it was Goya's home that would be remembered as the famous Quinta del Sordo.) Goya's house had 22 acres of farmland and was a solid, pink-and-white brick and adobe structure. He paid 60,000 reales in cash for the house. That same year, at age 73, Goya began working with a new means of printing, lithography, which had hardly existed even a generation. It was a method that Goya enjoyed because it was quicker and less labor intensive than old-style etching.

Along with the move came a woman and child. She was Leocadia Zorilla de Weiss, and little is known about her. By all accounts, she was an attractive woman, perhaps in her early thirties. She had been previously married to a German-Jewish jeweler who lived in Madrid but from whom she was divorced. Their marriage had produced two sons. Dona Leocadia was an extremely distant "relative" of the woman that Goya's son, Xavier, married. When Goya and Dona Leocadia became friends is not known. In 1819, her daughter, Rosario, was five years old, and rumors claimed that Goya was her father. Maybe he was, but no real evidence exists to prove or disprove the claim. It was clear to those around Goya that "he loved her as if she were his own."[112] Of all the things Leocadia was known for at the time, it was for her sharp tongue. Yet how much could this have mattered to the aged and otherwise lonely Goya? He was deaf.

As the years passed, Spain began to put its war with the French behind her, yet the spirit of revolution continued to boil in the hearts of the Spanish. A new campaign for constitution arose with a fervor, forcing Ferdinand to bring back the 1812 constitution he had destroyed only five years earlier. This liberal change greatly limited the Spanish monarch's power. By 1822, the French returned to Spain, this time to support the Spanish monarch, not replace him. By summer 1823, the army of constitutional supporters had been defeated, and Ferdinand once again ruled with an iron fist, taking out his revenge on all who had challenged or betrayed him.

As for Goya, the previous years of conflict, political intrigues, invasion, war, civil war, rebellion, and liberalism were finally beginning to take their toll on him. For 30 years, dating back to the French Revolution, he had seen tragedy and suffering, the triumph of dictatorship, and the crushing of liberalism. He was losing his faith in humanity. He came to believe that man was inherently evil and destructive and that life was absurd and everything was folly. Wanting to protest against the failures of his world, the painter was driven to create a series of works so morbid, depressing, faithless, and existential, they would come to be known as *pinturas negras*, "the black paintings."

THE BLACK PAINTINGS

A frustrated and disenchanted Goya painted these dark works on the walls of his farmhouse outside Madrid between 1820 and 1823. They reveal, perhaps more than any other works he ever produced, the artist's detachment and disappointment

The uncertain symbolism of Goya's "black paintings" is apparent in his bizarre work, *Fantastic Vision*. It is unclear who the two flying people are, or more importantly, what they represent. What is the rider pointing to, and at what is the red-cloaked figure looking back at? Perhaps only Goya himself knew the answers to such questions.

with the ways of the modern world. He painted them only for himself, with no intentions of showing them to anyone. Obviously, by not producing them on canvas or as etchings but rather on the walls of his home reveals that he "never expected his paintings to be displayed in public."[113] They were his *own* private hell.

Yet the works would not remain private. The two-story house had a large rectangular room on each floor, measuring roughly 14 (4.3m) feet by 26 feet (7.9m), along with two additional, smaller rooms. Goya would produce his "black paintings" in the larger room on each floor. They were still on the walls of his home during the late 1860s, 40 years after his death. By 1873, the house was purchased by a baron who removed the paintings and placed them on canvas. Later, they were displayed publicly for the first time in Paris at the

Universal Exposition of 1878. In 1881, their owner delivered the works to the Spanish government, and they were soon installed in the Prado Museum where they remain today. It was at the Universal Exposition that several late nineteenth-century impressionists viewed them and thought them the works of a man ahead of his time. Many, however, thought them little more than the work of an absolute madman.

The subjects of the "black paintings" were often shrouded in symbolism and mystery. Others were direct and disturbing. *Fantastic Vision* has been interpreted as a magical scene depicting two people flying off toward a large rock dominated by a castle and village. Yet the strange painting may have been a symbol of ruined lives of many Spanish liberals following the return of Ferdinand to power. These political outcasts often fled to Gibraltar, the "rock" in the painting, to avoid persecution. Another work, *Fight with Cudgels* focuses on two male giants thrashing at one another while standing knee-deep in a dimly lit wheat field. Some have interpreted the work as depicting Adam and Eve's eldest sons, Cain and Abel. Others view it as a metaphor of the civil war in Spain that had recently racked Goya's homeland.

Then there is the picture of the biblical figure, *Judith*, who, according to the Old Testament, seduced and then killed an enemy general by cutting off his head. The painting is comprised with shades of thickly painted grays and chalky whites, the dim-faced Judith raising her weapon to the sky, preparing to strike a death blow. It is similar to twentieth-century works created by Pablo Picasso, revealing that Goya was producing art beyond his own time. Other works were more macabre and dark and certainly would have landed Goya in trouble if known to the public. One such painting would later be titled (Goya did not title any of these dark works) *The Witches' Sabbath*. It is a horrific, phantasmagoric work, with the dark silhouette of a devilish goat figure dominating the center of the painting while surrounded by the ghastly shapes of witches.

Yet it is not the goat that Goya means as the focus of the work: it is instead likely he intended that to be the frightening faces of the witches themselves. Again, this is a work produced by broad impressionistic brushstrokes.

On the wall opposite *The Witches' Sabbath* was a work known today as *Pilgrimage of St. Isidore*. Despite its religious title, the painting depicts horrible-looking people, perhaps pilgrims, who are moving across a dark, stark landscape, stacked upon one another. Once again, the faces of the pilgrims tell the story Goya intended: that the emotionalism of the masses is brutal, shortsighted, and destructive. It has no connection to the individual will or the rational thought of the introspective. All is chaos and mindless folly.

Yet for all the ghastly scenes found amid Goya's "black paintings," the most lurid, disquieting, and brutally charged is *Saturn Devouring a Son*. The painting drew the anger of English artist and critic, P.G. Hamerton, who was driven by rage to write: "Of all these things the most horrible is the Saturn. He is devouring one of his children with the voracity of a famished wolf, and not a detail of the disgusting feast is spared you. The figure is a real inspiration, as original as it is terrific, and not a cold product of mere calculating design."[114] The subject matter of the grotesque painting, which shows a wild-eyed, long-haired, naked male figure eating the bloodied body of one of his young (the head and right arm have already been eaten off and Saturn is tearing with his teeth at the left arm) was one from Roman mythology. The Roman god Saturn, who wanted to reign without fear and challenge, made certain of his future power by devouring his own children. The work is so straight-forward and unblinking, it disgusts and spellbinds at the same time. The "son" in the painting is small, almost doll-like, for the body is not a child's but a diminutive version of an adult's form. That form is not of a male, however, but "a fragile female body."[115] Here, in this painting, the viewer gains an insight into "Goya's own demoniacal inner world."[116]

Goya's *The Milkmaid of Bordeaux*, painted when the master was 81 years old, marks the end of the artist's brilliant, innovative, and passionate career. Even in failed health, Goya's sketchy brushwork and light tones create a new direction in the world of art. Many critics credit *Milkmaid* as being a precursor to the French impressionism that began in the 1860s.

A NEW HOME IN BORDEAUX

By 1823, an elderly, tired Goya made an important decision. Concerned about his own safety in the Spanish court and in Spain in general, he handed his House of the Deaf Man over to his 17-year-old grandson, Mariano, and made preparations to leave his homeland. By spring the following year, Goya requested permission from the court to go to France, claiming he needed to take in the hot springs at Plombières, in southern France, for his health, "as his doctors have advised him."[117] The king granted permission almost immediately. Yet Goya never went to Plombières. He went to Bordeaux, which he reached on June 24. Bordeaux had become a city of exile for several of Goya's friends during the previous decades of war, invasion, and political intrigue, including Godoy's former wife, the duchess of Chinchon; Pepita Tudo, his naked maja; and the dukes of San Fernando and San Carlos.

In Bordeaux, he was received into the house of an old friend, Leandro Moratin, a poet and playwright, who noted that Goya appeared to him, "deaf, old, feeble, weak, not knowing a word of French, but so happy and eager to see the world."[118] That Goya was tired is clear. He was a man of the world, a world that had seen much chaos, violence, and blood. The elderly Spaniard was seeking shelter from the storms of life as well as "release from concern with the world of political and social intrigue, release from the demands of patrons and the importunings of acquaintances."[119]

Yet Goya did not remain in Bordeaux long. Within days of his arrival, he was off to Paris, where he arrived on June 20, 1824. The great painter had become a tourist in a foreign land. There is no record of Goya's reactions to the French capital, but he did find the time to paint another bullfight picture and a pair of portraits of another friend, Joaquin Maria Ferrer, and his wife. He also completed a straightforward self-portrait with pen and ink in which the artist wears a simple cap and coat, appearing as little more than a weary traveler. A light seems to have gone out.

Goya returned to Bordeaux by September and soon settled down in a small house with a garden. His friend Leocadia Weiss and her daughter, Rosario, came to join him. The artist was not finished with his work, however, and began once again applying himself to the new printing technique of lithography. To this end, he produced four famous lithographic plates titled the *Bulls of Bordeaux*. The works were almost experimental for Goya, who not only applied the new printing technique to his work but produced the end results using "crayons, a razor, and a scraper to achieve highly original effects of form and color."[120]

Life in Bordeaux did bring Goya the desired release and escape from a world he had come to nearly despise in his old age. He had complete freedom, painting a portrait of his friend Moratin and otherwise enjoying life. Moratin would later write of the elderly Spanish master: "He likes the city, the countryside, the climate, the food, and the independence and tranquility which he can enjoy."[121] He was enjoying his time with young Rosario, now 10 years old, who was to the artist his greatest delight. She seems to have had some talent as an artist. She and Goya drew together and painted miniatures, a new artistic outlet for the aged Aragonese painter. From time to time, Goya became ill during his stay at Bordeaux, and Moratin thought he might die. Goya was diagnosed with paralysis of the bladder. He developed a large tumor on the bone of one of his legs.

In 1826, when Goya turned 80, he made a visit to his native Spain where he paid a call in Madrid. He probably visited with his son, Xavier, and his grandson while there, but he made the trip to renew his official permissions to remain in France as well as request retirement as Court Painter. In the great Spanish city that had spurred so much of Goya's art throughout the decades, the court painter who had succeeded him, Vicente Lopez, painted Goya's portrait. The work was commissioned by King Ferdinand himself, who treated Goya with kindness and respect. The king not only renewed his permission for the artist to remain in Bordeaux, he also granted him a pension of 50,000 reales a year. When Goya finally left Madrid to return to France, it would not be his last. He would return again in summer 1827, the last time he would see his homeland. The reason for that final visit is unknown.

THE END OF HIS DAYS

The last years of Goya's life were spent peacefully and leisurely. Following his visit to Madrid, Moratin wrote about how his friend was doing: "Goya is fine. He keeps busy with his sketches, he walks, eats, takes his siestas; it seems that right now peace reigns over his hearth."[122] He drew a wide variety of sketches, including several based on his visit to the Bordeaux insane asylum. He produced, even as his life approached its end, yet another great masterpiece, *The Milkmaid of Bordeaux.* The work became rumored as his last painting, even though it was not so. Perhaps his subject was actually Rosario, but no one really knows. The painting symbolizes Goya's final years. It is a simple painting of a simple young woman. She is lovely and innocent, glancing pensively away from the viewer. Goya creates with this work an uncluttered and small canvas. There is nothing but the milkmaid—no milk pail, no animals, and no landscape—who presents to the viewer no allegory, no mystery, no symbolism, no overadorned royalty, no political essay, no satire on human depravity, and no story worth telling, except to Goya.

The year 1828 would be Goya's last. In February, he requested his grandson, Mariano, along with his wife, to pay him a visit in Bordeaux. They arrived the following month. In a letter Mariano wrote to his father, Grandfather Goya added a few lines of his own: "I can only say that I have become a little indisposed with so much happiness, and am in bed. God grant that I may see you come to see them [his family], for that would make my pleasure complete."[123]

Xavier made the trip to Bordeaux, but he dawdled, spending too much time in Paris, and he arrived too late. On the morning of April 2, the aged artist woke up, discovering that in his sleep he had lost the ability to speak and that his side had become paralyzed. In the days that followed, he regained his speech, but his paralysis did not leave him. For nearly two weeks, he struggled. In a letter written later by Dona Leocadia to Goya's friend in Bordeaux, Moratin, she described the artist's end:

> Thus he was for 13 days. . . . He would look at his hand, but as if stupefied; he wanted to make a will, he said, in our favor, and his daughter-in-law replied that he already had. After that he was not out of danger for a moment . . . weakness impeded the limited understanding of what he said, and he rambled . . . he died at about 2 in the morning on the night of the 15th–16th . . . so serenely, and departed as one asleep; even the doctor was astonished at his courage; he said he did not suffer at all, but I am not so sure of that![124]

THE AFTERMATH OF GOYA'S DEATH

Following a stroke on April 2, 1828, Goya managed to live two more weeks until he died on April 16. Through those weeks, he fell into a coma and was speechless and unresponsive. A handful of people waited at his bedside, including his companion, Dona Leocadia.

The distribution of Goya's estate was important. There were many paintings and sketches in his collection and his estate. The vast majority of his property and belongings went to Xavier. A small portion went to his friend Mariano. All this was distributed under a will that Goya had written up in 1811. The will was written so that it could not be changed, meaning that his companion for more than a decade, Dona Leocadia, was left nothing.

Xavier did give Dona Leocadia something, despite his strong personal dislike for her. She was allowed to take some of Goya's furniture, household linens, and clothing. She was also offered 1,000 francs to help cover the costs of returning to Spain with her daughter. Xavier did not allow her to remain in the house where Goya died.

With the passing of Goya, the world of Western art found itself in the throes of change, much of which had been brought on by the life's work of the Spanish artist himself. All things neoclassical or baroque had long ago vanished from the artistic landscape of Europe. They were replaced by an advancing tide of romanticism, to which Goya had been one of its most important and earliest contributors. That Goya had lived a long, full life as an artist may well be an understatement, of course. That Goya had seen much tragedy, pain and suffering is clear. He had witnessed events too grotesque, too gruesome, and too dark for most artists to even try to capture on canvas, but the Spanish artist had approached it all unflinchingly, having managed to, in the words of the poet Baudelaire, capture "the black magic of our civilization."[125]

Xavier gave Dona Leocadia a single painting, *Milkmaid of Bordeaux*. The work may have been based on a portrait of her daughter, Rosario. Yet Dona Leocadia did not keep the painting for long. By the following year, living in poverty, she was driven to sell the work to a distant relative of Goya's, Juan Bautista de Muguiro.

Goya's body would not remain in France. By 1901, the Spanish government made an official request to have Goya's body removed and given to Spain for reburial in his homeland. Permission was granted, and, before year's end, the remains were sent to Madrid and reburied.

The story does not end there, however. In 1929, officials decided to have Goya reburied again, this time beneath the floor of the Church of Santa Maia de la Florida, where Goya had painted his lovely angelic frescoes. During the exhumation, Goya's century-old body was examined and found to be missing its skull. No one has ever explained the reason for the artist's missing head.

Chronology

1746   Francisco Goya born March 30 in Fuendetodos near Saragossa, Spain.

1763   Arrives in Madrid.

1770   Makes trip to Italy to see great Renaissance works. Receives honorable mention in art competition held by the Academy of Fine Arts in Parma.

1771   Returns to Saragossa and receives commissions for a series of works for the Sobradiel Palace's chapel in Saragossa.

1773   Marries Josefa Bayeu, sister of the successful painter and influence on Goya, Francisco Bayeu. Paints frescoes for the Charterhouse of Aula Dei while in Saragossa.

1774   Commissioned by the Royal Tapestry Factory of Santa Barbara to produce designs for tapestry productions. Living in Madrid.

1746
Francisco Goya born March 30 in Fuendetodos near Saragossa, Spain

1773
Marries Josefa Bayeu

1786
Appointed Painter to the King

1746

1786

1774
Commissioned by the Royal Tapestry Factory of Santa Barbara to produce designs for tapestry productions

1780
Unanimously elected to membership of the Royal Academy of Fine Arts in San Fernando

1763
Arrives in Madrid

1780 Unanimously elected to membership of the Royal Academy of Fine Arts in San Fernando.

1783 Commissioned by Spanish royal minister, count of Floridablanca, to paint his portrait. Paints additional aristocratic portraits, including the duke and duchess of Osuna.

1784 Francisco Xavier is born, the only child who will survive into adulthood.

1786 Appointed Painter to the King and receives an annual salary of 15,000 reales.

1789 A year following the death of Carlos III, is appointed Court Painter by Carlos IV. Revolution breaks out in France.

1792 Goes deaf. Produces the last of his tapestry cartoons. Manuel Godoy becomes prime minister.

1789
**Appointed
Court Painter
by Carlos IV**

**1799
Publishes
The Caprices,
a collection
of 80 dark
etchings**

**1828
Dies on April 16
and is buried in
France**

1789   1828

**1795
Appointed Director
of the Royal
Academy. Paints
famous portrait,
*The Duchess
of Alba***

**1812
Wife,
Josefa, dies**

**1814
Paints two great
works to com-
memorate Spanish
uprising against
the French, *The
Second of May
1808* and *The
Third of May 1808***

1793 At work in Madrid, while in France, Louis XVI is beheaded by French revolutionaries. France declares war on Spain.

1795 Appointed Director of the Royal Academy. Paints famous portrait, *The Duchess of Alba.*

1796–1797 Visits the newly widowed duchess of Alba at her estate in Andalusia. There, he paints another portrait of her wearing black and begins work on *The Caprices.*

1798 Paints portrait of the minister Jovellanos as well as frescoes for the chapel of San Antonio de la Florida.

1799 Publishes *The Caprices,* a collection of 80 dark etchings. Appointed First Court Painter with an annual salary of 50,000 reales. Napoleon comes to power in France.

1800 After long preparations and sketches, paints the family of Carlos IV.

1802 Duchess of Alba dies suddenly.

1804 Napoleon crowns himself emperor of France.

1806 Mariano, Goya's grandson is born.

1807 The French invade Spain.

1808 Prime Minister Godoy is removed from office, and Carlos IV is forced to abdicate his throne. His son, Ferdinand VII, is also forced to resign and goes into exile. On May 2 and 3, street demonstrations and riots in Madrid are dealt with harshly by the French.

1810 Begins work on a series of etchings later titled *The Disasters of War.* Paints portrait of Joseph Bonaparte, who has been placed on the throne of Spain by his brother.

1812 Wife, Josefa, dies.

1814 War with France ends with the abdication of Napoleon. King Ferdinand returns to the Spanish throne. Paints two great works to commemorate the conflict, *The Second of May 1808* and *The Third of May 1808.*

1816   Publishes collection of bullfighting aquatints.

1819   Buys a house, the Quinta del Sordo. Struggles with numerous illnesses.

1820–1823   Secretly decorates the walls of two rooms in his house with the "black paintings."

1824   Granted permission to move to France where he takes up residence in Bordeaux.

1826   Returns to Madrid briefly and during his visit, King Ferdinand VII grants him an annual pension of 50,000 reales.

1827   Visits Spain one last time. After returning to Bordeaux, he paints *The Milkmaid of Bordeaux.*

1828   Dies on April 16 and is buried in France.

Notes

Introduction

1. Quoted in Robert Hughes, *Goya* (New York: Alfred A. Knopf, 2003), 261.
2. Ibid.
3. Ibid., 248.
4. Ibid., 253.
5. Ibid., 254.
6. Ibid.

Chapter 1

7. Quoted in Evan S. Connell, *Francisco Goya: Life and Times* (New York: Counterpoint Publishers, 2004), 6.
8. Ibid.
9. Quoted in Richard Schickel, *The World of Goya, 1746–1828* (New York: Time-Life Books, 1968), 13.
10. Ibid.
11. Ibid.
12. Connell, 7.
13. Schickel, 9.
14. Connell, 7.
15. Schickel, 11.
16. Ibid., 13.
17. Ibid., 14.
18. Ibid.
19. Ibid.
20. Connell, 13.

Chapter 2

21. Ibid., 14.
22. Ibid.
23. Quoted in Claus Virch, *Francisco Goya* (New York: McGraw-Hill Book Company, 1967), 8.
24. Schickel, 15.
25. Connell, 15.
26. Schickel, 30.
27. Ibid., 31.
28. Connell, 20.
29. Schickel, 35.
30. Ibid., 36.
31. Ibid., 37.
32. Ibid.

Chapter 3

33. Ibid., 38.
34. Virch, 8.
35. Schickel, 39.

Chapter 4

36. Ibid., 49.
37. Ibid., 50.
38. Ibid., 51.
39. Ibid.
40. Quoted in Janis Tomlinson, *Francisco Goya y Lucientes, 1746-1828* (London: Phaidon Press, Ltd., 1994), 25.
41. Virch, 12.
42. Tomlinson, 27.
43. Ibid.
44. Ibid.
45. Ibid., 16.
46. Schickel, 55.
47. Ibid., 51.

Chapter 5

48. Ibid., 55.
49. Ibid.
50. Ibid., 56.
51. Ibid.
52. Ibid., 57.
53. Ibid., 50.
54. Ibid.
55. Ibid., 57.
56. Ibid.
57. Ibid., 58.
58. Ibid.
59. Ibid.
60. Quoted in Jeannine Baticle, *Goya: Painter of Terrible Splendor* (New York: Harry N. Abrams, Inc., Publishers, 1994), 40.
61. Schickel, 59.
62. Ibid., 78.
63. Ibid., 79.
64. Baticle, 46.

Chapter 6

65. Ibid., 48.
66. Ibid., 51.
67. Ibid., 57.

68. Ibid.
69. Ibid.
70. Tomlinson, *Goya*, 78.
71. Schickel, 85.
72. Baticle, 64.
73. Schickel, 86.
74. Baticle, 58.
75. Ibid., 64.
76. Quoted in Sarah Carr-Gomm, *Francisco de Goya, 1746–1828* (Kent, England: Grange Books, 2005), 82.
77. Baticle, 66.
78. Ibid.

Chapter 7
79. Ibid., 67.
80. Schickel, 97.
81. Ibid.
82. Ibid., 98.
83. Ibid.
84. Ibid.
85. Hughes, 131.
86. Schickel, 98.
87. Ibid., 100.
88. Connell, 1
89. Baticle, 72.
90. Ibid., 76–77.
91. Hughes, 214.
92. Baticle, 78.

Chapter 8
93. Ibid., 84.
94. Ibid.
95. Quoted in Rose-Marie and Rainer Hagen, *Francisco Goya, 1746–1828* (Los Angeles: Taschen, 2003), 29.

96. Ibid.
97. Schickel, 72.
98. Tomlinson, *Goya,* 164.
99. Schickel, 127.
100. Ibid., 126.
101. Baticle, 91.
102. Ibid., 91–92.
103. Schickel, 127.
104. Ibid.

Chapter 9
105. Baticle, 94.
106. Virch, 43.
107. Tomlinson, 197.
108. Baticle, 112.
109. Hughes, 313.
110. Virch, 45.

Chapter 10
111. Baticle, 113.
112. Schickel, 167.
113. Quoted in Fred Licht, *Goya: The Origins of the Modern Temper in Art* (New York: Harper & Row, Publishers, 1983), 159.
114. Virch, 46.
115. Baticle, 119.
116. Virch, 46.
117. Hughes, 389.
118. Baticle, 124.
119. Schickel, 166.
120. Baticle, 124.
121. Schickel, 170.
122. Hughes, 400.
123. Schickel, 171.
124. Ibid.
125. Ibid.

Bibliography

Baticle, Jeannine. *Goya: Painter of Terrible Splendor.* New York: Harry N. Abrams, Inc., 1994.

Brown, Jonathan. *Goya's Last Works.* New Haven, Conn.: Yale University Press, 2006.

Carr-Gomm, Sarah. *Francisco de Goya, 1746-1828.* Kent, England: Grange Books, 2005.

Connell, Evan S. *Francisco Goya: Life and Times.* New York: Counterpoint Publishers, 2004.

Hagen, Rose-Marie, and Rainer Hagen. *Francisco Goya, 1746–1828.* Los Angeles: Taschen, 2003.

Hofmann, Werner. *Goya: "To Every Story There Belongs Another."* New York: Thames & Hudson, 2003.

Hughes, Robert. *Goya.* New York: Alfred A. Knopf, 2003.

Licht, Fred. *Goya: The Origins of the Modern Temper in Art.* New York: Harper & Row, Publishers, 1983.

Rishel, Joseph. *Goya, Another Look.* Philadelphia: Philadelphia Museum of Art, 1999.

Schickel, Richard. *The World of Goya, 1746–1828.* New York: Time-Life Books, 1968.

Tomlinson, Janis. *Francisco Goya y Lucientes, 1746–1828.* London: Phaidon Press, Ltd., 1994.

———. *From El Greco to Goya: Painting in Spain, 1561–1828.* New York: Harry N. Abrams, Inc., 1997.

Virch, Claus. *Francisco Goya.* New York: McGraw-Hill Book Company, 1967.

Further Reading

Gudiol, Jose. *Goya.* New York: Harry N. Abrams, Inc., 1989.

Muhlberger, Richard. *What Makes a Goya a Goya?* New York: Viking Children's Books, 1994.

Sanchez, Alfonso Perez. *Goya.* New York: Henry Holt & Company, Inc., 1990.

Schiaffino, Maria Rosa. *Goya.* Grand Rapids, Mich.: School Specialty Publishing, 1990.

Venezia, Mike. *Francisco Goya.* New York: Scholastic Library Publishing, 1991.

Wright, Patricia *Goya.* New York: DK Publishing, Inc., 1993.

WEB SITES

WebMuseum, Paris
www.ibiblio.org/wm/paint/auth/goya/

CyberSpain
www.cyberspain.com/passion/goya.htm

Francisco Goya
www.imageone.com/goya/index.html

Metropolitan Museum of Art/Timeline of Art History
www.metmuseum.org/toah/hd/goya/hd_goya.htm

Famous Painter.com
www.famouspainter.com/goya.htm

Napoleonic Guide/Goya's Disasters of War
www.napoleonguide.com/goyaind.htm

Picture Credits

page:

Index

Index

About the Author

TIM McNEESE is associate professor of history at York College in York, Nebraska, where he is in his sixteenth year of college instruction. McNeese earned an associate of arts degree from York College, a bachelor of arts in history and political science from Harding University, and a master of arts in history from Missouri State University. A prolific author of books for elementary school, middle school, high school, and college readers, McNeese has published more than 90 books and educational materials over the past 20 years, on everything from Salvador Dali to the settling of Santa Fe. His writing has earned him a citation in the library reference work, *Contemporary Authors*. In 2006, McNeese appeared on the History Channel program, *Risk Takers, History Makers: John Wesley Powell and the Grand Canyon*. He was a faculty member at the 2006 Tony Hillerman Mystery Writers Conference in Albuquerque, where he presented on the topic of American Indians of the Southwest. His wife, Beverly, is an assistant professor of English at York College. They have two children, Noah and Summer, and two grandchildren, Ethan and Adrianna. Tim and Bev sponsored study trips for college students on the Lewis and Clark Trail in 2003 and 2005. Readers may email Professor McNeese at tdmcneese@york.edu.